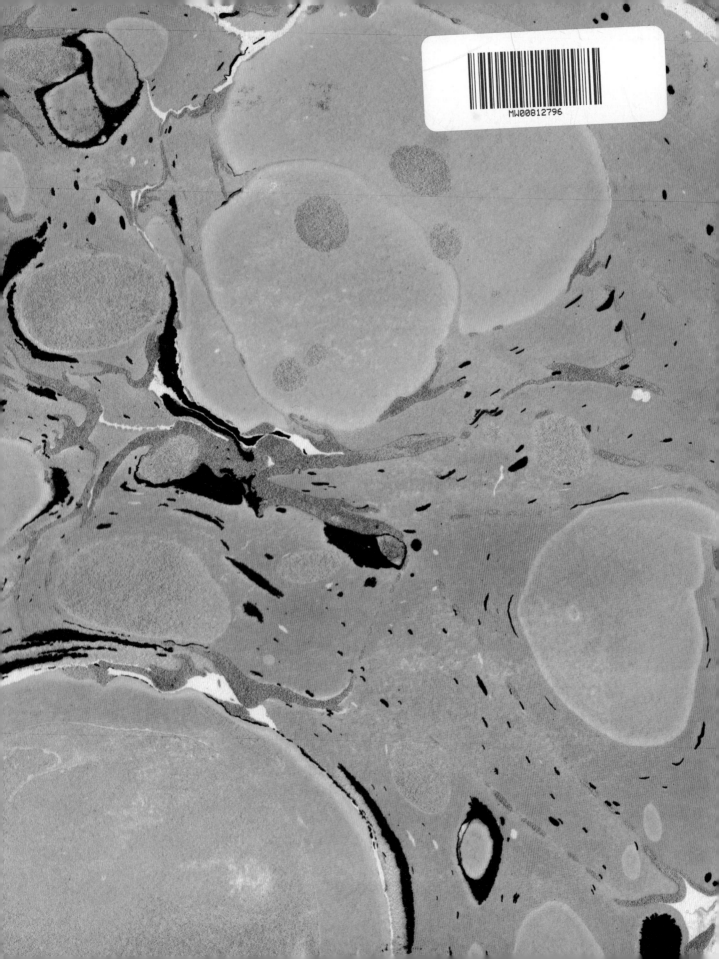

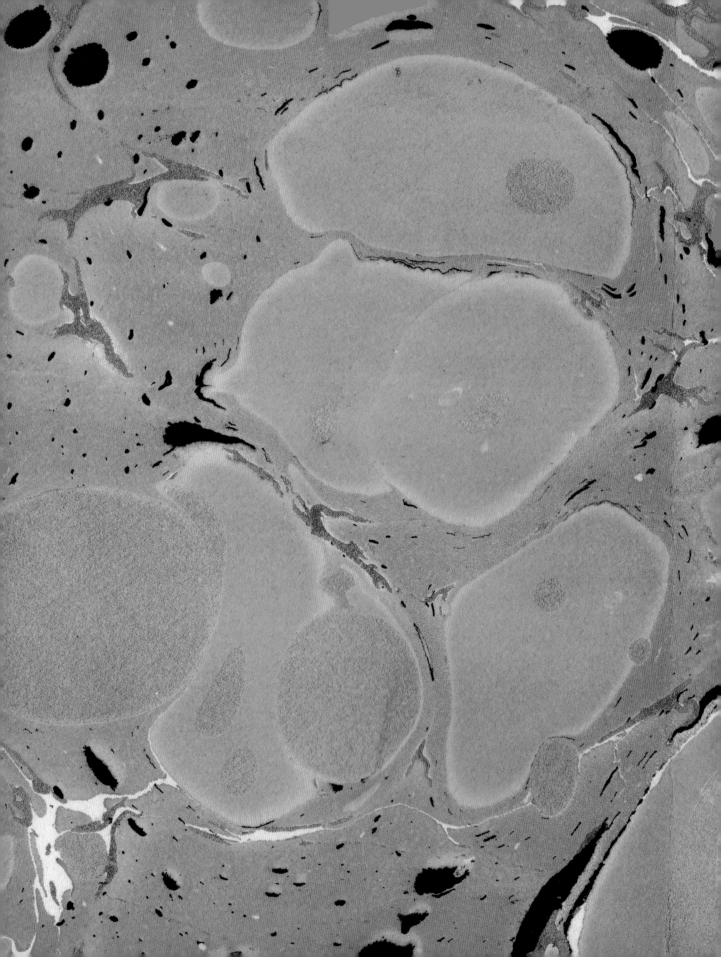

ALSO BY NICOLE RUCKER

Dappled

Fat + Flour

Fat + Flour

THE ART OF A SIMPLE BAKE

Nicole Rucker

ALFRED A. KNOPF   NEW YORK   2025

THIS IS A BORZOI BOOK PUBLISHED BY ALFRED A. KNOPF

www.aaknopf.com

Knopf, Borzoi Books, and the colophon are registered trademarks of Penguin Random House LLC.

Library of Congress Cataloging-in-Publication Data
Names: Rucker, Nicole, author.
Title: Fat + flour : the art of a simple bake / Nicole Rucker.
Description: First edition. I New York : Alfred A. Knopf, 2025. I Includes index.
Identifiers: LCCN 2024007806 (print) I LCCN 2024007807 (ebook) I
ISBN 9780593801789 (hardcover) I ISBN 9780593801796 (ebook)
Subjects: LCSH: Desserts. I Baking. I Pastry. I Cooking (Fruit) I LCGFT: Cookbooks.
Classification: LCC TX773 .R844 2025 (print) I LCC TX773 (ebook) I DDC 641.7/1—dc23/eng/20240228
LC record available at https://lccn.loc.gov/2024007806
LC ebook record available at https://lccn.loc.gov/2024007807

Some of the recipes in this book may include raw eggs, meat, or fish. When these foods are consumed raw, there is always the risk that bacteria, which is killed by proper cooking, may be present. For this reason, when serving these foods raw, always buy certified salmonella-free eggs and the freshest meat and fish available from a reliable grocer, storing them in the refrigerator until they are served. Because of the health risks associated with the consumption of bacteria that can be present in raw eggs, meat, and fish, these foods should not be consumed by infants, small children, pregnant women, the elderly, or any persons who may be immunocompromised. The author and publisher expressly disclaim responsibility for any adverse effects that may result from the use or application of the recipes and information contained in this book.

Cover design by Anna B. Knighton
Cover photograph by Alan Gastelum

Manufactured in China
First Edition

THIS BOOK IS DEDICATED TO

YOU.

YOU DESERVE A SWEET TREAT.

01
Cookies

02
Brownies and Bars

03
Bundt and Loaf Cakes

04
Five Distinct Banana Bread Recipes

05
Fruit Pies, Handpies, Galettes

06
Pudding and Custard Pies

A few years ago, I fell out of love with baking.

That's not a great thing for a professional baker—and perhaps not the most promising way to begin a book about baking, but it's true. I was blindsided by the feeling when it arrived.

I'd opened a bakery, Fat + Flour, in 2019, with a few friends and colleagues helping me a few days a week. Together we worked out of an under-the-counter fridge and a tiny half-sized electric oven. We made truly small batches of cookie dough out of a stand mixer not much larger than a home model. All for the love of the baking.

Then the entire world came to a standstill as coronavirus landed in all of our laps. Here came a new hurdle, a massive hurdle, even when we thought it was only going to be a two-week inconvenience. It felt big and terrifying. Baking felt futile.

As the pandemic continued on, in never-ending roller-coaster-style ups and downs, my objective became clearer than ever: STAY OPEN. I was so tired, and stressed out, and scared . . . Everyone was. We knew nothing, remember? Every week began to feel like Thanksgiving prep week, which, if you have ever worked in a bakery, you know is like the Super Bowl and boot camp smashed into one crazy day. It is a mountain of work and organization, and if you are lucky, a few moments of accomplishment and joy. But now baking felt like a chore. I decided to close for a few weeks, get some rest, and try to process the uncertainty of the future. I needed some space from baking.

Meanwhile, everyone I knew was baking at home. To pass the time, to feel something other than dread, to soothe their souls with banana bread. During the first week I stayed home, I baked nothing, took up paper marbling, thought about becoming a mystery novelist, and started a journal. (Both paper marbling and journaling have since been abandoned; I still dream of writing a mystery novel.)

By the second week, though, I was making drop biscuits nearly every day. They were so easy, a recipe I had been making and rewriting since I was a teenager. An unfussy, all-purpose, nourishing baked good that was low-effort but high-reward. I posted the recipe on social media, and friends and strangers thanked me for reminding them that they could make something so simple and still feel that spark of joy you get when you make something well. That's the kind of recipe I found myself wanting.

Gradually, baking started to feel like something I needed to do again. I started to miss baking pies, but I didn't miss making pie dough—my very hands-on recipe felt like a chore—and *that* was when I had the spark of energy to turn all my recipes on their sides and change everything. Why *wasn't* I using a stand mixer to mix my pie dough? Why *does* every cookie recipe in my recipe binder start with "cream butter and sugar together until light and fluffy"? Why *can't* every recipe be as simple to put together as a good banana-bread recipe?

What started out as a shortcut became what I now call the Cold Butter Method, CBM, which has become a catalyst for a streamlined baking process that I put

Introd

to use both at home and at work. It was inspired by the vintage cake-baking techniques referred to as the "reverse creaming method" and the "double-quick method" of beating softened butter into the dry ingredients before introducing any liquid. I wondered why I wasn't using cold butter in the same fashion to get the desired effect of larger broken-down pieces of butter amongst butter-coated flour. If this worked with cakes, could I use this method to bypass creaming butter for a cookie recipe? (Spoiler alert: YES.)

I began to strip away some of the airs and fuss of baking on a larger scale, and tinkered with home baking in a way I never had before. There I was—forty years old, back in the kitchen, finding myself in a bowl of smashed banana guts. Some people were discovering sourdough; I was on a journey to rediscover the love I'd once had for the craft with which I had made my name. I ended up discovering an entirely different way of thinking about baking, both at home and at work.

That is what this book is about.

As I worked through a few of my favorite recipes, looking at old habits and rules that had forced me into a rut, I realized that, as I moved forward, a core value of my baking life would be to not fuck around with fussiness unless it's 100 percent necessary. One of the things that has made me the happiest during this exploration was finding smarter ways to work while still baking THE BEST of something.

The result is this book. *Fat + Flour* is a celebration of the unadorned joy that mixing these two simple ingredients together can bring.

Not every recipe in this book uses CBM, but all of them are designed in answer to a few core questions: Are all these steps necessary? Are all these tools necessary? What is the best and simplest path to the desired outcome? Answering these questions and writing unfussy, delicious recipes became a calling for me, and through that work the love has returned.

Developing these recipes has brought me so much joy and freedom in my kitchen, which is what I wish for everyone who makes them. I have written them with care, in the hopes that any time the thought "I want to bake something" enters your mind, you will look to this book and know that it will guide you to an unfussy but exceptional cookie, cake, bar, or pie. →

About the Recipes

When writing this book, I worked strictly from my home kitchen. These recipes have been tested both by bakers with standard home ovens and by those with convection ovens. For anyone unfamiliar with convection, this simply means that the heat source is aided by hot air circulated by a fan, usually on the back wall of the oven. It has a few benefits: faster and more even browning, and shorter cooking times overall. At temps higher than 400°F, a convection oven creates a lot of beautiful caramelization on meats and vegetables, but it can burn baked goods easily if the recipe is not adjusted. I am fortunate that I get to use a convection oven both at work and at home, and even though I prefer using a convection setting for everything in this book, every recipe works with either kind. The temperature given in each recipe is for a standard home oven without convection. For those using a convection oven, I suggest you reduce the cooking time by 25 percent to start, and watch for the signs of doneness.

Each recipe gives more than one indication of doneness; if you look for those signs as well as watch the timer, you will have success. This is especially important when baking fruit and custard pies. In my years of experience with pie, most of my baking errors occurred when I second-guessed the timer and ignored the signs of doneness—undercooking fruit pies can mean a soupy mess, and overcooking custard pies can result in scrambled sweet eggs. Sometimes the margin of perfection for a chocolate-chip cookie is forty-five seconds—which is why you'll find me standing with my hand on the oven door handle waiting for the timer.

About the Measurements

These recipes were developed using the professional standard, the metric system (mostly). That means the larger measurements are weighed in grams. But the smaller measurements, such as salt and spices, are measured with U.S. teaspoons and tablespoons, because the kitchen scales most people have at home cannot register measurements smaller than five grams with accuracy.

I love using the metric system, and I hope you are already a gram convert; if not, maybe this will be a gentle nudge toward purchasing a scale and getting on board! I have included the U.S. standard measurements alongside the grams because I want everyone to use this book, and also because, every once in a while, I get a little lazy and use a deli cup to measure things by volume.

Quick Conversions

All-purpose flour	125g (1 cup)
Brown sugar, packed	213g (1 cup)
Granulated sugar	200g (1 cup)
Turbinado sugar	180g (1 cup)
Diamond Crystal kosher salt	3g (1 teaspoon)
Baking soda	6g (1 teaspoon)
Baking powder	4g (1 teaspoon)
Vanilla extract	5g (1 teaspoon)
Butter	113g (4 ounces, 8 tablespoons, ½ cup)
Neutral cooking oil	198g (1 cup)
Rolled oats	90g (1 cup)
Almond flour	96g (1 cup)

325°F = 162°C
350°F = 176°C
375°F = 190°C
400°F = 204°C
3 teaspoons = 1 tablespoon
4 tablespoons = ¼ cup

Essential Kitchen Tools

Very few tools are required to make the recipes in this book, but here are a few that I view as indispensable.

Baking sheets At least two sizes for a well-stocked kitchen. I recommend a commercial half sheet pan (12.9 by 17.9 inches) and a quarter sheet pan (9 by 13 inches), both made of pure aluminum. This type of baking sheet has a high-grade thickness, so it's very sturdy and doesn't warp or bend easily. It conducts heat well and evenly, and is the professional standard for baking. A quarter sheet is a good size to use for freezing cookie-dough balls before baking, and is also the perfect size for a batch of brownies. The half sheet pan is the ideal size for baking six average-sized cookies, or more if the style of cookie is smaller.

Stand mixer or hand mixer Most of the recipes in this book can be made using a hand mixer and a tall-sided mixing bowl. Some of the recipes (such as pie dough) are more easily prepared using a stand mixer. In my opinion, a stand mixer gives more bang for your buck if you are an avid baker, and is a kitchen tool that can last a very long time (fifteen years at least).

Cake pans Nordic Ware makes my preferred loaf and Bundt cake pans; they are nonstick and made of solid aluminum. The nonstick coating is great, but still needs to be coated before baking, especially if you plan to use any of the extra fluted and decorative styles. For the Sunken Fruit Cake on page 94, I use a 9-by-12-inch Le Creuset casserole dish.

Digital scale Buy one; you won't regret it. If you are able to find one that can accurately measure small quantities of an ingredient (+/- 1g), then you have struck gold. Since many American kitchen scales are not as reliable at micro-measurements, I cite teaspoons and tablespoons for things like salt and spices.

Measuring cups For liquid, I like a glass Pyrex measuring cup, or a clearly lined OXO plastic measuring cup. For measuring dry ingredients, I prefer to use a scale, but if you absolutely need a set of measuring cups, please use those designed for dry ingredients only—they are typically metal, have handles, and come as a set.

Measuring spoons I like a measuring spoon that is made of metal and allows for a nice clean swipe across the top to level the surface of the ingredient you're measuring.

Mixing bowls This is a category of tool that I could easily get lost describing—I have very specific mixing-bowl needs. For me, the ideal all-purpose mixing bowl is narrow at the base, can hold at least five liters, has tall sides, and has a pouring spout. Usually, I prefer glass, so I can see the bottom of what I am mixing. Most of my baking is still done at work, and the standard stainless-steel mixing bowl used in every restaurant kitchen is undeniably handy and affordable. They are also lighter than glass and ceramic, which makes them easier to handle, and they come in MANY sizes.

01

Cookies

I once had a business partner who during a slow sales season proclaimed,

"Cookies are a public service—cookies aren't paying the bills." I took this personally, even though in that particular business cookies were definitely not paying many bills. I agree with him partially: a great cookie from your local café or bakery is something of a community perk. But if you dip just a finger into the vast world of cookies, you will find that they are a bit of a bully in the dessert universe. They rule the scene. Sure, cakes and pies are very popular, but cookies? Cookies are IT.

Many families have their own cherished cookie recipes that date back generations. I have a friend who sends a group text message proclaiming the start of the holiday season every year with a pic of her family recipe for polvorones. Even in a non-baking family like mine, cookies were often homemade.

Because I'm a bit of a recipe-history enthusiast, something that has always interested me is the vast array of chocolate-chip cookies. The fact that a recipe developed as late as 1938 has become ubiquitous, with millions of recipes published and more coming every day, is remarkable and makes my job of baking and writing recipes even more fun. There are five versions in this book, and it was difficult to stop myself there. What I decided on was to show the range of subcategories: classic, thin and crisp, thick and gooey, nutty, and, my favorite of them all, the 1990s Oatmeal Chocolate Chunk Cookie (page 6). And if chocolate isn't your favorite cookie ingredient, do not fear: there are twelve other recipes to inspire a quick bake session.

Today, at my own bakery, we typically offer between six and twelve different kinds of cookies every day. Cookies, at last, are literally paying the bills. ∎

The **Cold Butter Method**

Cold Butter Method, or CBM as I call it, is a streamlined way of bringing together a batter that skips the tempering step for the butter. Cold fat is worked into the dry ingredients before introducing the wet ingredients. This method saves time and removes the ever present question of just how much to cream the butter. The result is a dough or batter that comes together quickly and has a tender crumb.

Combine the dry ingredients (flour, sugar, leavening, salt, spices) for the recipe in the bowl of your stand mixer. Mix briefly with the paddle attachment on low speed. Add the cubed cold butter to the dry ingredients and mix on low speed until the butter has been broken down and the mixture resembles damp, rustic sand. Add any chocolates, nuts, or other add-ins the recipe calls for, and briefly mix on low speed to disperse them. Add the wet ingredients. Mix on low speed to combine, until all the dry bits have been incorporated and you have a cohesive cookie dough. Proceed with the recipe's portioning and baking instructions as written. ∎

1990s Oatmeal Chocolate Chunk Cookies

1¼ cups (156g) unbleached
   all-purpose flour

½ teaspoon (3g) baking soda

½ teaspoon (1.5g) Diamond
   Crystal kosher salt

⅓ cup (30g) rolled oats

¼ cup + 1 tablespoon (62.5g)
   granulated sugar

½ cup + 2 tablespoons packed
   (133g) dark-brown sugar

4 ounces (113g) cold unsalted
   butter, cubed

1¼ cups (212.5g) roughly chopped
   72% chocolate chunks,
   + more for topping the
   dough balls before baking

1 large egg (50g)

1 teaspoon (5g) vanilla extract

Any bakery in America worth its sugar must have a signature chocolate-chip cookie recipe. I have worked my way through nearly every style of the genre over the years, and as I write this, at least, my preference is for a wrinkly, buttery, chocolate-chunk version. This style gives me memories of a very specific cookie served in my middle-school cafeteria between the years 1990 and 1992. It's got traditional bittersweet chocolate chunks rather than chips, oatmeal for texture, and a ratio of fat to flour that yields a perfect chew. Though the dough does get even better if left to age overnight in the fridge, 30 minutes in the freezer will do the trick if you just want to get on with your life and eat cookies. ▶

◀ In the bowl of a stand mixer fitted with the paddle attachment, mix the flour, baking soda, salt, oats, and sugars together, to disperse the soda and break up any lumps of sugar. Add the cold butter, and mix on low speed until the mixture resembles rustic sand, about 4 minutes. Add the chopped chocolate, and briefly mix on low speed to disperse it.

◀ Whisk the egg and vanilla together in a small bowl, and slowly add them to the stand mixer bowl, mixing on low speed. Once all the egg has been incorporated, turn the speed to medium to bring the dough together.

◀ Use a spoon to portion the dough into twelve balls, and transfer the portioned cookie dough to a plate or a quarter sheet pan. Add the extra chopped chocolate to the tops of all the dough balls, and freeze them, uncovered, for 30 minutes. While the dough chills, preheat your oven to 375°F (190°C). Line two half sheet pans with parchment.

◀ Place the balls of dough, six to each parchment-lined sheet pan, and bake both on the center racks of your oven for 7 minutes. Rotate the sheet pans, and continue baking for another 8 to 9 minutes, until the cookies are risen and browned at the edges, but soft and a bit wet-looking in the center. The cookies will continue to set up as they cool. Store any uneaten cookies in a sealed container in the fridge. For the best results, warm them for 15 seconds in the microwave to refresh them before eating. They are best eaten within 3 days.

When these chocolate-chip cookies are baked to perfection (browned edges, blond middle), they make great ice-cream sandwiches. Thanks to the brown sugar and the touch of oats, and to reducing the amount of flour just slightly, they stay nice and chewy when frozen. ■

1½ cups (187g) unbleached
   all-purpose flour

1 teaspoon (3g) Diamond
   Crystal kosher salt

½ teaspoon (3g) baking soda

1 teaspoon (4g) baking powder

⅓ cup + 1 tablespoon (79g)
   granulated sugar

½ cup packed (106g) dark-brown sugar

4 ounces (113g) cold unsalted
   butter, cubed

½ cup (85g) bittersweet chocolate
   chips, + more for topping the
   dough balls before baking

½ cup (85g) milk chocolate
   chips, + more for topping the
   dough balls before baking

¾ cup (85g) roughly chopped pecans,
   toasted, + more for topping the
   dough balls before baking

1 large egg (50g)

2 teaspoons (10g) vanilla extract

n the name of "All Cookies Are Good Cookies," I had to include an extra-thick chocolate-chip cookie, even though this style is not my go-to preference. But there is something about the size of a thick-style cookie that creates a perfect ratio of soft/gooey interior to browned exterior; the high ratio of flour to fat has a lot to do with that, as well as the higher baking temp, which sets the exterior of this hefty cookie quickly. If you are a fan of what bakers all over the world call the "NYC Style Cookie," then this might be your ideal.

Use caution while baking these cookies—do not go too far from the oven. The magic fudgy, warm interior results from removing what might look like barely set cookies from the oven—another 2 minutes will give you a soft, cakey cookie, but it won't have the same fudgy texture as a slightly underbaked one. ▶

◀ In the bowl of a stand mixer fitted with the paddle attachment, mix the flour, salt, baking soda, baking powder, and sugars together, to disperse the soda and powder and break up any lumps of sugar. Add the cold butter, and mix on low speed until the mixture resembles rustic sand, about 4 minutes. Add the chocolate chips and pecans, and briefly mix on low speed to disperse them.

◀ Whisk the egg and vanilla together in a small bowl, and slowly add them to the buttery mixture on low speed. Once all the egg has been incorporated, turn the speed to medium to bring the dough together. At this point, you may look at the dough and ask yourself if this is going to happen—it will, and just when it does come together, you must turn the machine off immediately or risk a tough cookie.

◀ Use a spoon to portion the dough into six mounds, but do not roll them into balls, and try not to compact them too much (this is key to the shape and texture of the cookie when it bakes). Add the decorative chocolate chips and nuts to the tops of each dough mound, transfer the dough to a plate or quarter sheet pan, and freeze them, uncovered, for 30 minutes. While the dough chills, preheat your oven to 375°F (190°C). Line two half sheet pans with parchment.

◀ Place the mounds of dough, three to each parchment-lined sheet pan, and bake them both on the center racks of your oven for 10 minutes. Rotate the sheet pans, and continue baking for another 6 to 8 minutes, until the cookies are risen and browned at the edges, but soft and a bit wet-looking in the center. *Underbaking* this cookie is crucial. Because of the thickness of the dough, they will continue cooking and "setting" after you remove them from the oven. Let them cool for 15 minutes after removing them from the oven before eating them warm. They are best eaten the same day, but you can store any uneaten cookies in a sealed container in the fridge. For the best results, warm them for 15 seconds in the microwave to refresh them before eating.

Fat and Gooey Chocolate Chunk Cookies with Pecans

East Coast Crunch Cookies

MAKES 24 SMALL CRISPY COOKIES

4 ounces (113g) unsalted butter, cubed

2 teaspoons (10g) vanilla extract

1 cup (125g) unbleached all-purpose flour

1 teaspoon (6g) baking soda

⅓ cup (66g) granulated sugar

½ cup packed (106g) light-brown sugar

2 teaspoons (5g) instant chicory powder

1 teaspoon (3g) Diamond
    Crystal kosher salt

1 large egg white (33g)

¼ cup (42g) finely chopped
    72% chocolate chunks

There is a specific type of small, crispy cookies that are sold at grocery stores. You've probably had them; they come in green paper bags. They are kind of my nemesis. I've spent an hour making a homemade dessert, only to have my husband reach into the cupboard and grab a few of these after dinner—the ultimate burn for a pastry chef. My ego bruised, I knew an homage (I would never say "copycat version," because no one can ever truly achieve the specific flavor of these mass-produced crispy, buttery cookies) to the Tate's cookie was necessary. My personal touch is a bit of instant chicory and a heavy hand with the salt. This recipe uses melted butter for texture; breaking down the fat and adding it to the batter in a liquid form reduces the amount of aeration in the batter, and when it's cooling, the texture of the cookie compacts significantly. This, combined with a higher proportion of white sugar to encourage the spreading of the dough, makes the finished cookie a pleasingly crunchy facsimile. ▶

◀ **Brown the butter** Place it in a small saucepan over medium heat. Bring it to a simmer, and continue cooking, stirring frequently, until the butter begins to foam and brown. Once it's browned, remove the butter from the heat, and pour it into a large heatproof bowl to cool. Add the vanilla right away to stop the cooking; it might sputter a little, so be careful. Allow the browned butter to come to room temperature.

◀ Measure the flour and baking soda into a small bowl, and whisk them together.

◀ Add the sugars, chicory powder, and salt to the browned butter, and whisk to bring them together. Add the egg white, and whisk vigorously until the mixture is pale and thick, about 45 seconds. Add the flour and chopped chocolate to the butter-and-egg mixture, and fold it in, until a dough comes together. Use a spoon to portion the dough into twenty-four small mounds, about 25g each, gently rolling them to form smooth balls. Transfer the portioned dough balls to a plate or quarter sheet pan, and freeze them, uncovered, for 30 minutes.

◀ While the dough chills, preheat your oven to 375°F (190°C). Line two half sheet pans with parchment. Place the balls of dough, twelve to a sheet pan, giving them plenty of space to spread, and bake them both on the center racks of your oven for 10 minutes. Rotate the sheet pans, and bake for an additional 5 to 6 minutes, until the cookies are flat and browned. Remove the cookies from the oven and let them cool completely—they will not be crispy until they are totally cooled. Stored at room temperature in a sealed container, they stay crisp for about a week.

Finely chopped chocolate is a must, or else you will have big lumps of chocolate chips suspended in crispy dough. OK, that doesn't sound awful, but I prefer the finer chop dispersed throughout the cookie. The baking of these can also be tricky, as you are pushing the color to the very edge of browned. Then, when you remove them from the oven you have to wait at least an hour for them to be fully cooled or they won't be crispy. ∎

2 cups (250g) unbleached
   all-purpose flour

⅔ cup packed (142g) light-brown sugar

¼ cup (50g) granulated sugar

1 teaspoon (6g) baking soda

1 teaspoon (3g) Diamond
   Crystal kosher salt

1 tablespoon (10g) cornstarch

4 ounces (113g) cold unsalted
   butter, cubed

1⅓ cups (226g) bittersweet chocolate
   chips, + more for topping the
   dough balls before baking

1 large egg (50g)

1 large egg yolk (14g)

2 teaspoons (10g) vanilla extract

1 tablespoon (12g) neutral cooking oil

When I am craving a cookie that has a soft light-brown sugar profile, I turn to this recipe. It's a time-traveling sensory experience, taking me back to the late 1980s, when the most reliable chocolate-chip cookie was either made from the Nestlé Toll House yellow-bag recipe or the Pepperidge Farm Soft Baked cookie sold on grocery-store shelves. The texture is SOFT, toothsome, and moist, but definitely not cakey. This is all thanks to a few key swaps to the old-school Toll House recipe—the addition of a bit of neutral oil and a small amount of cornstarch keeps the texture on these perfect for up to 1 week in a sealed container. It's rare to find a cookie that can do that, but here it is! ▶

◀ In the bowl of a stand mixer fitted with the paddle attachment, mix the flour, sugars, baking soda, salt, and cornstarch together, to disperse the soda and break up any lumps of sugar. Add the cold butter, and mix on low speed until the mixture resembles rustic sand, about 4 minutes. Add the chocolate chips, and briefly mix on low speed to disperse them.

◀ Whisk the egg, egg yolk, vanilla, and oil together in a small bowl, and slowly add this to the buttery mixture on low speed. Once all the egg has been incorporated, turn the speed to medium to bring the dough together.

◀ Use a spoon to portion the dough into twelve balls, add the decorative chocolate chips to the tops of each dough ball, transfer them to a plate or a quarter sheet pan, and freeze them, uncovered, for 30 minutes.

◀ While the dough chills, preheat your oven to 375°F (190°C). Line two half sheet pans with parchment. Place the balls of dough, six to each parchment-lined sheet pan, and bake them both on the center racks of your oven for 10 minutes. Rotate the sheet pans, and bake for an additional 5 to 6 minutes, until the cookies are lightly browned at the edges and set but damp-looking in the center. Remove the cookies from the oven, and let them cool for a few minutes before eating them. Remarkably, several friends said these cookies tasted even better after 2 days, but they weren't in my kitchen eating them warm from the oven, so what do they know? Store any uneaten cookies in a sealed container in the fridge for up to a week. For the best results, warm them for 15 seconds in the microwave to refresh them before eating.

Classic Soft Chocolate Chip Cookies

Vegan Bourbon Chocolate Pecan Cookies

1½ cups (187g) unbleached
   all-purpose flour

1 teaspoon (6g) baking soda

1 teaspoon (3g) Diamond
   Crystal kosher salt

⅓ cup (66g) granulated sugar

½ cup packed (106g) dark-brown sugar

4 ounces (113g) cold unsalted
   vegan butter

2 tablespoons (20g) Bob's Red
   Mill egg replacer mixed with
   4 tablespoons cold water

1 tablespoon (14g) bourbon

2 teaspoons (10g) vanilla extract

¾ cup (85g) roughly chopped pecans,
   toasted, + more for topping the
   dough balls before baking

½ cup + 1 tablespoon (100g) vegan
   chocolate chips, + more for topping
   the dough balls before baking

W hen we first started making these cookies at Fat + Flour, we were shocked by how many people barely acknowledged the little "V" marking the sign in the pastry case. Sometimes vegan options get the side-eye, but this quickly became our most popular cookie. Customers always look shocked to be told that it's vegan, typically followed by "No way!" I have deduced that it is all in the name—it's got those hit words "bourbon," "chocolate," and "pecan," which jump out at people as they skip right past the little "V" indicating the cookie is vegan. Whatever the reason, these cookies are fantastic and much loved. One of the secrets is actually the result of its veganness: the vegan butter and lack of eggs make for a short dough that melds with the higher amount of brown sugar to create a cookie that is wonderfully crisp at the edges and chewy in the middle—the holy grail for any chocolate-chip cookie recipe. ▶

◀ In the bowl of a stand mixer fitted with the paddle attachment, mix the flour, baking soda, salt, and sugars together, to disperse the soda and break up any lumps of sugar. Add the cold butter, and mix on low speed until the mixture resembles rustic sand, about 4 minutes.

◀ Add the hydrated egg replacer to the buttery mixture, along with the bourbon and vanilla. Mix on low speed. Once all the wet ingredients have been incorporated, add the pecans and chocolate chips, and mix on medium speed to bring the dough together.

◀ Use a spoon to portion the dough into twelve balls, add the extra chopped pecans and chocolate chips to the tops of all the dough balls, transfer them to a plate or a quarter sheet pan, and freeze them, uncovered, for 30 minutes.

◀ While the dough chills, preheat your oven to 375°F (190°C). Line two half sheet pans with parchment. Place the balls of dough, six to each parchment-lined sheet pan, and bake them both on the center racks of your oven for 10 minutes. Rotate the sheet pans, and bake for an additional 5 to 6 minutes, until the cookies are lightly browned at the edges and set but damp-looking in the center. Remove the cookies from the oven, and let them cool for a few minutes before eating them. Store any uneaten cookies in a sealed container in the fridge for up to a week. For the best results, warm them for 15 seconds in the microwave to refresh them before eating.

2 cups (250g) unbleached
    all-purpose flour

⅔ cup packed (142g) light-brown sugar

¼ cup (50g) granulated sugar

1 teaspoon (6g) baking soda

1 teaspoon (3g) Diamond
    Crystal kosher salt

1 tablespoon (10g) cornstarch

4 ounces (113g) cold unsalted
    butter, cubed

1 large egg (50g)

1 large egg yolk (14g)

2 teaspoons (10g) vanilla extract

1 teaspoon instant espresso
    powder (optional)

1 tablespoon (12g) neutral cooking oil

1⅓ cups (225g) white-chocolate
    chips, + more for topping the
    dough balls before baking

½ cup (62g) roughly chopped
    macadamia nuts, + more for topping
    the dough balls before baking

This cookie is a grown-up version of the classic 1990s white-chocolate macadamia cookie, with espresso added to temper the sweetness of the white chocolate, and a little extra salt to amplify the butterscotch notes of the cookie base. Of course, other nuts would fit right in to substitute for the macadamia nuts, which can be a pricey addition. ▶

◀ In the bowl of a stand mixer fitted with the paddle attachment, mix the flour, sugars, baking soda, salt, and cornstarch together, to disperse the soda and break up any lumps of sugar. Add the cold butter, and mix on low speed until the mixture resembles rustic sand, about 4 minutes.

◀ Whisk the egg, egg yolk, vanilla, espresso powder, and oil together in a small bowl, and add this to the buttery mixture on low speed. Once all the wet ingredients have been incorporated, add the chocolate and nuts, and mix on medium speed to bring the dough together.

◀ Use a spoon to portion the dough into twelve balls, add the extra chocolate chips and nuts to the tops of each dough ball, transfer the dough to a plate or a quarter sheet pan, and freeze, uncovered, for 30 minutes.

◀ While the dough chills, preheat your oven to 375°F (190°C). Line two half sheet pans with parchment. Place the balls of dough, six to each parchment-lined sheet pan, and bake them both on the center racks of your oven for 10 minutes. Rotate the sheet pans, and bake for an additional 5 to 6 minutes, until the cookies are puffy and set at the edges. The centers will look cooked but when lightly touched on top will have a subtle squish. Remove the cookies from the oven, and let them cool for a few minutes before eating them. Store any uneaten cookies in a sealed container in the fridge for up to a week. For the best results, warm them for 15 seconds in the microwave to refresh them before eating.

Espresso and White Chocolate Cookies

Classic Chewy Sugar Cookies

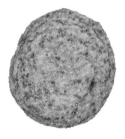

1¼ cups (218g) unbleached
    all-purpose flour

½ teaspoon (2g) baking powder

¾ cup (150g) granulated sugar

3 tablespoons packed (40g)
    light-brown sugar

1 teaspoon (3g) Diamond
    Crystal kosher salt

4 ounces (113g) cold unsalted
    butter, cubed

1 large egg (50g)

1 teaspoon (5g) vanilla extract

Coarse sugar or sprinkles, for rolling
    the cookies in (optional)

T hese are a classic, just as the name proclaims. This recipe comes from the longtime Fat + Flour baker Krystle Shelton, and has been the jumping-off point for many cookie recipes. The ratio of sugar to butter is crucial for a soft, chewy, but not too sweet sugar cookie, and this recipe balances those elements in harmony. ▶

◀ In the bowl of a stand mixer fitted with the paddle attachment, mix the flour, baking powder, sugars, and salt together, to disperse the baking powder and break up any lumps of sugar. Add the cold butter, and mix on low speed until the mixture resembles rustic sand, about 4 minutes.

◀ Whisk the egg and vanilla together in a small bowl, and add this to the buttery mixture on low speed. Once all the wet ingredients have been incorporated, mix on medium speed to bring the dough together.

◀ Put the sugar or sprinkles into a small bowl if you're using them to decorate the cookies. Use a spoon to portion the dough into twelve balls, roll each one in sugar or sprinkles, then transfer them to a plate or quarter sheet pan. Freeze the portioned cookie dough for 30 minutes.

◀ While the dough chills, preheat your oven to 375°F (190°C). Line two half sheet pans with parchment. Place the balls of dough, six to each parchment-lined sheet pan, and bake them both on the center racks of your oven for 10 minutes. Rotate the sheet pans, and bake for an additional 5 to 6 minutes, until the cookies are puffy and set at the edges. The centers will look cooked but when lightly touched on top will have a subtle squish. Remove the cookies from the oven, and let them cool for a few minutes before eating them. Store any uneaten cookies in a sealed container in the fridge for up to a week. For the best results, warm them for 15 seconds in the microwave to refresh them before eating.

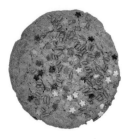

1¾ cups (218g) unbleached
   all-purpose flour

½ teaspoon (2g) baking powder

¾ cup (150g) granulated sugar

3 tablespoons packed (40g)
   light-brown sugar

1 teaspoon (3g) Diamond
   Crystal kosher salt

4 ounces (113g) cold unsalted
   vegan butter, cubed

2 tablespoons (20g) Bob's Red
   Mill egg replacer mixed with
   4 tablespoons cold water

1 teaspoon (5g) vanilla extract

Coarse sugar or sprinkles, for rolling
   the cookies in (optional)

Handling the ups and downs of food cost is an ever-annoying part of managing any small business, but sometimes spikes can unexpectedly inspire changes to the menu in positive ways. When the weird post-Covid market threw the prices of both butter and eggs into unmanageable territory, I decided to commit to switching a portion of my cookie recipes to vegan and eliminate the pricey animal products cutting into the bottom line. No one noticed except vegans, who were glad to have a delicious cookie. ▶

◀ In the bowl of a stand mixer fitted with the paddle attachment, mix the flour, baking powder, sugars, and salt together, to disperse baking powder and break up any lumps of sugar. Add the cold vegan butter, and mix on low speed until the mixture resembles rustic sand, about 4 minutes.

◀ Whisk the egg replacer and vanilla together in a small bowl, and add this to the buttery mixture. Mix on low speed. Once all the wet ingredients have been incorporated, mix on medium speed to bring the dough together.

◀ Put the sprinkles or sugar into a small bowl if you're using them to decorate the cookies. Use a spoon to portion the dough into twelve balls, roll each one in sugar or sprinkles, then transfer them to a plate or quarter sheet pan. Freeze the portioned cookie dough for 30 minutes.

◀ While the dough chills, preheat your oven to 375°F (190°C). Line two half sheet pans with parchment. Place the balls of dough, six to each parchment-lined sheet pan, and bake them both on the center racks of your oven for 10 minutes. Rotate the sheet pans, and bake for an additional 5 to 6 minutes, until the cookies are puffy and set at the edges. The centers will look cooked but when lightly touched on top will have a subtle squish. Remove the cookies from the oven, and let them cool for a few minutes before eating them. Store any uneaten cookies in a sealed container in the fridge for up to a week. For the best results, warm them for 15 seconds in the microwave to refresh them before eating.

Vegan Soft and Rich Sugar Cookies

Snickerdoodle Cookies

For the Cookies

1¾ cups (218g) unbleached
  all-purpose flour

2 teaspoons (8g) ground cinnamon

½ teaspoon (2g) cream of tartar

¼ teaspoon (1.5g) baking soda

½ teaspoon (1.5g) Diamond
  Crystal kosher salt

½ cup (100g) granulated sugar

⅓ cup packed (71g) light-brown sugar

7 ounces (198g) cold unsalted
  butter, cubed

1 tablespoon (14g) unrefined
  extra-virgin coconut oil

1 large egg (50g)

1 large egg yolk (14g)

2 teaspoons (10g) vanilla extract

For the Cinnamon Sugar

⅓ cup (66g) granulated sugar

2 teaspoons (8g) ground cinnamon

Pinch of Diamond Crystal kosher salt

didn't grow up eating snickerdoodles, but when I opened my own bakery they became one of the most requested cookies, so of course I had to create my own version. As with all classic cookies, people argue about what makes a snickerdoodle a snickerdoodle. For me, the defining properties are a pillowy and tender cookie made with cream of tartar and dredged in cinnamon sugar. Some recipes do not consider cream of tartar a crucial element, but I found that the tangy flavor it imparts, and the very specific leavening characteristics it creates, yield a superior version to those made with baking powder. The coconut oil in the recipe creates an extra-soft-at-room-temperature crumb that I think takes this snickerdoodle over the top. ▶

◀ **Make the cookies** In the bowl of a stand mixer fitted with the paddle attachment, mix the flour, cinnamon, cream of tartar, baking soda, salt, and sugars together, to disperse the soda and break up any lumps of sugar. Add the cold butter and coconut oil, and mix on low speed until the mixture resembles rustic sand, about 4 minutes.

◀ Whisk the egg, egg yolk, and vanilla together in a small bowl, and add this to the buttery mixture. Mix on low speed. Once all the wet ingredients have been incorporated, mix on medium speed to bring the dough together.

◀ **Make the cinnamon sugar** Whisk the sugar, cinnamon, and salt together in a small bowl.

◀ Use a spoon to portion the dough into twelve balls, roll each ball in the cinnamon sugar, and transfer them to a plate or quarter sheet pan. Freeze the portioned cookie dough for 30 minutes.

◀ While the dough chills, preheat your oven to 375°F (190°C). Line two half sheet pans with parchment. Place the balls of dough, six to each parchment-lined sheet pan, and bake them both on the center racks of your oven for 10 minutes. Rotate the sheet pans, and bake for an additional 5 to 6 minutes, until the cookies are puffy and set at the edges. The centers will look cooked but when lightly touched on top will have a subtle puffy, squishy give. Cool the cookies for 15 to 20 minutes before eating. Store any uneaten cookies in a sealed container in the fridge for up to a week. For the best results, warm them for 15 seconds in the microwave to refresh them before eating.

Pumpkin Snickerdoodle Cookies

MAKES 12 COOKIES

For the Pumpkin

½ cup (125g) pumpkin purée

For the Cookie Dough

1¾ cups (218g) unbleached all-purpose flour

¼ teaspoon (1g) baking powder

¼ teaspoon (1.5g) baking soda

½ cup (100g) granulated sugar

½ cup packed (106g) dark-brown sugar

½ teaspoon (1.5g) Diamond Crystal kosher salt

1 tablespoon (12g) pumpkin pie spice

4 ounces (113g) cold unsalted butter, cubed

2 large egg yolks (28g)

1 teaspoon (5g) vanilla extract

For the Spiced Sugar

1 cup (200g) granulated sugar

2 teaspoons (8g) pumpkin pie spice

Pinch of Diamond Crystal kosher salt

I love summer fruits, but there gets to be this time in Los Angeles between mid-August and mid-September when the heat gets so bad and everyone gets grumpy and starts longing for Fall and Winter. That first week of Summer Hell is when I start plotting the pumpkin bakes, looking toward cooler temps and my chance to bust out this perfect pumpkin cookie. ▶

◀ **Blot the pumpkin** The secret to the texture of this cookie is removing some of the water from the pumpkin purée. I do this by measuring the purée and placing it on a double layer of paper towels, covering it with another double layer of paper towels, and pressing down lightly, to blot the surface gently, so the paper begins to absorb the excess moisture. I leave the pumpkin in the paper until I'm ready to add it to the batter, but typically for no longer than 10 minutes.

◀ **Make the cookie dough** In the bowl of a stand mixer fitted with the paddle attachment, mix the flour, baking powder, baking soda, sugars, salt, and spice together, to disperse the soda and powder and break up any lumps of sugar. Add the cold butter, and mix on low speed until the mixture resembles rustic sand, about 4 minutes.

◀ Add the pumpkin, egg yolks, and vanilla to the buttery mixture. Mix on low speed until all the pumpkin has been incorporated and you have a thick dough. Chill the dough for 30 minutes before portioning.

◀ Preheat your oven to 375°F (190°C). Line two half sheet pans with parchment.

◄ **Make the spiced sugar** Whisk together the sugar, pumpkin pie spice, and salt in a small bowl.

◄ Use a spoon to portion the chilled dough into twelve equal balls, then roll them in the spiced sugar. Place the balls of dough, six to each parchment-lined sheet pan, and bake them both on the center racks of your oven for 10 minutes. Rotate the sheet pans, and bake for an additional 5 to 6 minutes, until the cookies are puffy and set at the edges.

◄ Remove the cookies from the oven, and rap the pan on the counter to settle them before leaving them to cool for 15 minutes. They are best eaten warm the same day, but, thanks to the pumpkin purée, these cookies are still amazing 2 days later. Store any uneaten cookies in a sealed container in the fridge. For the best results, warm them for 15 seconds in the microwave to refresh them before eating.

Boozy Banana Snickerdoodle Cookies

MAKES **12** COOKIES

For the Banana

½ cup (125g) mashed ripe banana

For the Cookie Dough

1¾ cups (218g) unbleached all-purpose flour

¼ teaspoon (1g) baking powder

¼ teaspoon (1.5g) baking soda

½ cup (100g) granulated sugar

½ cup packed (106g) dark-brown sugar

½ teaspoon (1.5g) Diamond Crystal kosher salt

1 tablespoon (12g) ground cinnamon

4 ounces (113g) cold unsalted butter, cubed

1 cup (114g) roughly chopped pecans or walnuts, toasted

2 large egg yolks (28g)

1 teaspoon (5g) vanilla extract

1 tablespoon (14g) bourbon

For the Cinnamon Sugar

1 cup (200g) granulated sugar

2 teaspoons (8g) ground cinnamon

¼ teaspoon Diamond Crystal kosher salt

I can't quite remember what provoked me to make this recipe in the first place, but I am pretty sure it was a late-night altered-state question, such as, "What if the sugary top of the best banana bread was baked in cookie form, delivering a peak banana-bread experience in every bite?" That's what this LOOSE adaptation of a snickerdoodle is. Once I had created an ideal pumpkin snickerdoodle, why not go all the way to cozy and spin it in a banana direction? These cookies are soft, spicy, and aromatic with cinnamon, vanilla, and bourbon. ▶

◀ **Blot the banana** Measure the mashed banana, place it on a double layer of paper towels, cover it with another double layer of paper towels, and gently blot the banana so the paper begins to absorb the excess moisture. Leave the banana in the paper until you're ready to use it.

◀ **Make the cookie dough** In the bowl of a stand mixer fitted with the paddle attachment, mix the flour, baking powder, baking soda, sugars, salt, and cinnamon together, to disperse the soda and powder and break up any lumps of sugar. Add the cold butter, and mix on low speed until the mixture resembles rustic sand, about 4 minutes.

◀ Add the nuts, banana, egg yolks, vanilla, and bourbon to the buttery mixture. Mix on low speed until all the banana has been incorporated and you have a thick dough. Chill the dough for 30 minutes before portioning.

◀ Preheat your oven to 375°F (190°C). Line two half sheet pans with parchment.

◄ **Make the cinnamon sugar** Whisk together the sugar, cinnamon, and salt in a small bowl.

◄ Use a spoon to portion the chilled dough into twelve equal balls, then roll them in the spiced sugar. Place the balls of dough, six to each parchment-lined sheet pan, and bake them both on the center racks of your oven for 10 minutes. Rotate the sheet pans, and bake for an additional 5 to 6 minutes, until the cookies are puffy and set at the edges.

◄ Remove the cookies from the oven, and rap the pan on the counter to settle them before leaving them to cool for 15 minutes. They are best eaten warm the same day, but, thanks to the banana purée, these cookies are still amazing 2 days later. Store any uneaten cookies in a sealed container in the fridge. For the best results, warm them for 15 seconds in the microwave to refresh them before eating.

1½ cups (187g) unbleached
    all-purpose flour

1 teaspoon (6g) baking soda

½ cup (45g) rolled oats

⅔ cup (133g) granulated sugar

¼ cup packed (53g) dark-brown sugar

1 teaspoon (3g) Diamond
    Crystal kosher salt

2 tablespoons (18g) coconut-milk powder

1 teaspoon (4g) ground
    cinnamon (optional)

4 ounces (113g) cold unsalted
    butter, cubed

1 tablespoon (14g) unrefined
    extra-virgin coconut oil

1 large egg (50g)

1 teaspoon (5g) vanilla extract

½ cup (46g) shredded unsweetened
    coconut, + more for rolling the cookies

W hen I'm workshopping new recipes, coconut is often at the top of my ingredient list. There's just something about it, probably the buttery and nutty flavor, that really calls to me—so much so that I have to stop myself from adding it to every recipe. Just know that, if you love coconut, I see you. This chewy coconut cookie delivers a warm balance of brown sugar, vanilla, and coconut notes with a good amount of cinnamon for coziness. The secret to its texture is a higher amount of granulated sugar, for crispiness and to encourage the cookie to spread, and a touch of coconut oil, to create a buttery texture and an added layer of coconut flavor. Some people will be angry about the cinnamon; if that's you, then leave it out. ▶

◀ In the bowl of a stand mixer fitted with the paddle attachment, mix the flour, baking soda, oats, sugars, salt, milk powder, and cinnamon together, to disperse the soda and break up any lumps of sugar. Add the cold butter and coconut oil, and mix on low speed until the mixture resembles rustic sand, about 4 minutes.

◀ Whisk the egg and vanilla together in a small bowl, and slowly add this to the buttery mixture, on low speed. Once all the egg has been incorporated, add the shredded coconut, and turn the speed to medium to bring the dough together.

◀ Use a spoon to portion the dough into twelve balls, roll them in coconut, and transfer the dough balls to a plate or quarter sheet pan. Freeze the portioned cookie dough for 30 minutes. While the dough chills, preheat your oven to 375°F (190°C). Line two half sheet pans with parchment.

◀ Place the balls of dough, six to each parchment-lined sheet pan, and bake them both on the center racks of your oven for 10 minutes. Rotate the sheet pans, and bake for an additional 5 to 6 minutes, until the cookies are risen and browned at the edges, but soft and a bit wet-looking in the center. Remove the cookies from the oven, and rap the pan on the counter to settle them before leaving them to cool for 15 minutes. They are best eaten warm the same day, but still amazing 2 days later. Cool any uneaten cookies completely, and store them in a sealed container.

Chewy Coconut Oatmeal Cookies

Triple Chocolate Cookies

1½ cups (187g) unbleached
 all-purpose flour

½ cup (42g) Dutch-processed
 cocoa powder

1 teaspoon (4g) baking powder

½ teaspoon (3g) baking soda

1 teaspoon (3g) Diamond
 Crystal kosher salt

½ cup (100g) granulated sugar

½ cup packed (106g) dark-brown sugar

4 ounces (113g) cold unsalted
 butter, cubed

1 large egg (50g)

1 large egg yolk (14g)

2 teaspoons (10g) vanilla extract

½ cup (85g) 72% chocolate
 chunks, + more for topping the
 dough balls before baking

½ cup (85g) white-chocolate
 chunks, + more for topping the
 dough balls before baking

One of the fun things about owning my own bakery is spotting customer trends and preferences. These cookies are definitely a deep, dark experience, and I noticed as soon as we put them on the menu that many of the European travelers coming through the market would dive into a Triple Chocolate Cookie for breakfast, often buying them in multiples after having a single cookie with some espresso. I love this—I love watching people find their "thing" that calls to them from the pastry case. We use white chocolate as the third "chocolate" in the title, but they're great with milk-chocolate chunks as well. ▶

◀ In the bowl of a stand mixer fitted with the paddle attachment, mix the flour, cocoa powder, baking powder, baking soda, salt, and sugars together, to disperse the soda and powder and break up any lumps of sugar. Add the cold butter, and mix on low speed until the mixture resembles rustic sand, about 4 minutes.

◀ Whisk the egg, egg yolk, and vanilla together in a small bowl, and slowly add this to the buttery mixture on low speed. Once all the wet ingredients have been incorporated, add the chocolate chunks, and mix on medium speed to bring the dough together.

◀ Use a spoon to portion the dough into twelve balls, add the extra chocolate chunks to the tops of all the dough balls, transfer the dough balls to a plate or quarter sheet pan, and freeze them, uncovered, for 30 minutes. While the dough chills, preheat your oven to 375°F (190°C). Line two half sheet pans with parchment.

◀ Place the balls of dough, six to each parchment-lined sheet pan, and bake them both on the center racks of your oven for 10 minutes. Rotate the sheet pans, and bake for an additional 5 to 6 minutes, until the cookies are puffy and set at the edges. The centers will look cooked but, when lightly touched on top, will have a subtle squish. Remove the cookies from the oven, gently but firmly rap the pan three times on the counter to spread the hot cookies a little bit, and let them cool for a few minutes before eating them. Store any uneaten cookies in a sealed container in the fridge for up to a week. For the best results, warm them for 15 seconds in the microwave to refresh them before eating.

5 ounces (140g) silken tofu

¼ cup (49g) grapeseed oil
or other neutral oil

½ cup (100g) granulated sugar,
+ more for rolling the cookies

¼ cup packed (50g) light-brown sugar

1 teaspoon (5g) vanilla extract

¼ cup (21g) Dutch-processed
cocoa powder

1 teaspoon (3g) Diamond
Crystal kosher salt

1 teaspoon (4g) baking powder

1½ cups (187g) unbleached all-
purpose flour or gluten-free flour

¾ cup (127g) dark chocolate
chunks, vegan if you prefer

O ne of the first places I started cooking and baking was a place called Che Café Collective in San Diego, a music venue on the campus of UCSD that has become a legendary stop for many bands since its founding in 1980. It remains open to all who want to volunteer, no matter age or experience. I was in high school when I started volunteering at the Che, mostly to get free entrance into concerts, and made lifelong friends there, including Nichole Kreglow, who organized volunteers and bands during the late 1990s. One of the best memories I have from my time there was being allowed to work in the kitchen, making vegan food with college students, especially this specific cookie, which we made from a book called *Tofu Cookery* by Louise Hagler. I have reworked the recipe to make it a little more indulgent, and updated it with modern ingredients.

Here is where I encourage you to look past the unconventional addition of silken tofu in a cookie recipe, because the texture it provides is like NOTHING ELSE. This is my favorite double-chocolate cookie; it happens to be vegan. ▶

◀ Preheat your oven to 375°F (190°C). Line two half sheet pans with parchment paper.

◀ In a blender, combine the tofu, oil, sugars, and vanilla. Blend until the mixture is smooth.

◀ Whisk together the cocoa powder, salt, baking powder, and flour in a large mixing bowl. Add the tofu mixture and chocolate chunks to the flour mixture, and use a spatula to combine everything into a stiff dough.

◀ Put some granulated sugar into a small bowl. Use a spoon to portion the dough into twelve equal balls, roll each one in sugar. Place the balls of dough, six to each parchment-lined sheet pan, and bake them both on the center racks of your oven for 10 minutes. Rotate the sheet pans, and bake for an additional 5 to 6 minutes, until the cookies are very puffy and bouncy when touched, but a bit wet-looking in the center. Cool the cookies for 15 to 20 minutes before eating. Store any uneaten cookies in a sealed container in the fridge for up to a week. For the best results, warm them for 15 seconds in the microwave to refresh them before eating.

Co-Op Tofu Brownie Cookies

Dutch-Processed Cocoa vs. Natural Cocoa

My goal is that all my recipes can be made well by anyone who wants to make them, home bakers and professionals alike. I often have two different testers work through new recipes to make sure they achieve the desired results. Sometimes they don't, and we have to investigate why. This was the case with the Co-Op Tofu Cookies (page 33). I will admit, this is a super-specific and possibly weird recipe (tofu with chocolate? sounds crazy), but when these cookies are made with the right ingredients they are GREAT—bouncy, squidgy, and deeply chocolatey.

That's where the cocoa comes in. The inspiration for this recipe is from a book written in the 1980s, when *natural* cocoa was the most common cocoa on the market. The original recipe also called for baking soda—a good match for natural cocoa, which is acidic, because the natural cocoa and the baking soda react to create tiny bubbles and texture in the cookie and the baking soda is neutralized in the process. When I tested the recipe at home, I was out of the fancier brand of cocoa I usually use and turned to Hershey's (natural) cocoa instead. I proceeded with the recipe and worked on a few iterations before passing it on to my friend and recipe tester Cindi Thompson, an excellent baker.

Cindi could not make these cookies to save her life. Each try was a flop. Dense, with no rise, they were like lumps of coal on a baking sheet. I was so confused, because they worked fine at my house. Cindi isn't the biggest chocolate-person, but she takes her job seriously, and after two failed attempts, she started to get mad about it. She assumed at first that she had measured wrong, gave it another try, and failed again. At this point, Cindi thought either she or the recipe was cursed.

Stubborn as I am, I knew there was a good reason for the disparity, and after a series of investigative questions, we realized the culprit—THE COCOA. Cindi, like many avid bakers these days, was using Dutch-processed cocoa. The process of "Dutching" removes much of the acidic properties of cocoa, smoothing the edges of its flavor and making it less reactive. Baking soda relies on the acidic properties of other ingredients, including natural cocoa, to react. When paired with the Dutch cocoa, it was giving . . . nothing. It also left a soapy flavor in the dense, failed cookies, since the baking soda had not been neutralized by an acid. Gross all around!

Once we figured it out, I had a choice to make. Stay true to the original recipe and use natural cocoa, or update it for modern times and use Dutch-processed cocoa. I chose to update, for several reasons: "specialty" ingredients have become increasingly available since the 1980s, and tastes have changed—we now look to the dark and smooth flavor of Dutch-processed cocoa as a sign of quality, and color. It's a purely aesthetic choice, but I prefer the darker color of Dutch-processed cocoa in my baked goods.

So—here we are, with a baking book written in what I call the Golden Age of Cocoa. For many recipes that call for cocoa and don't specify a type, such as brownie recipes, you can use your preferred cocoa ounce for ounce. Since brownies do not contain chemical leavening agents like baking soda or baking powder, either cocoa will yield edible (and probably delicious) results. For the rest of the cocoa recipes, as long as you remember a few rules, you can make swaps depending on what you have on hand.

In this book, I have specified which cocoa I would like you to use to get the intended flavor, color, and rise in each chocolatey recipe. But even I run out of my favorite brand sometimes and have to make adjustments on the fly. Here are the shorthand details and attributes of a few commonly found styles of cocoa and how they will act in a recipe:

Natural cocoa Light-brown–pinkish tone in color when baked. Cheaper options may contain less fat; look for a natural cocoa with at least 20 percent cocoa butter fat for flavor and texture. Has an acidic pH; if a reaction is needed in the recipe (cakey rise), it will probably be paired with baking soda.

Dutch-processed cocoa Dark-brown–deep-red-brown color when baked. May be advertised as "European" or "intense" because of its richer color and darker flavor. Dutch-processed cocoa is typically more expensive, the reason being that it is often made with higher-quality cocoa beans and retains a much higher fat content—sometimes twice as much cocoa butter fat than natural cocoa. Dutch processing reduces the natural acidity in cocoa, making it neutral, with a typical pH of 7; therefore, it will not react with baking soda. If a recipe calls for baking soda only, you should not substitute Dutch cocoa without adjusting the leavening. To use Dutch-processed cocoa in a recipe calling for natural cocoa and only baking soda, replace the *baking soda* with twice as much *baking powder*, and leave all other ingredient amounts the same.

Cocoa blend This trend is just now becoming popular, and I predict it will be the future of cocoa powder for home baking. Why not blend the best natural cocoa with the best Dutch-processed cocoa for a magical "middle" version that can be used in nearly any recipe? Because blends vary in consistency from maker to maker, it can be hard to pinpoint a standard pH level for a cocoa blend; it's best to consult the maker for more info if you're curious what the ratio of natural to Dutch cocoa is in any particular blend. Cocoa blends will never be as dark and rich as pure Dutch-processed, but they can provide extra oomph in flavor, texture, and acidity for recipes calling for natural cocoa and baking soda. You do not need to adjust your recipe to swap in a cocoa blend.

Black cocoa The darkest of the cocoas, black cocoa is just ultra-Dutch-processed and often uses darker-roasted cocoa. The extra Dutch processing further reduces the acidity in black cocoa, making it alkaline, with a pH of 8. It creates a dramatic effect when baked—the blackest of chocolate cakes, and that iconic Oreo-color cookie. The flavor can be polarizing: some people love it, some people (including me) think it doesn't taste like chocolate at all and that it's best used in a cake, where perhaps some chocolate frosting can do the heavy lifting in the flavor department. Black cocoa can range in fat content, so, if you find your only option is low-fat (10–12 percent), I would skip it and use a high-quality Dutch-processed cocoa with a higher fat content (20–25 percent).

Red cocoa / cocoa rouge I find red cocoa to be a happy medium in the Dutch-processed category. It provides an intense fudgy aroma and flavor, and a rich burgundy color after baking. If you choose to have just one type of cocoa on hand, a red cocoa is a good option. It has enough fat content to contribute deep flavor and moist texture, but its roast level doesn't compete with other flavors. Cocoa rouge is still emerging as a cocoa-powder offering, and, depending on the maker, the pH level can vary, but most of the brands making this type of cocoa powder note the pH at around 7–7.5. In recipes that need leavening, it needs acid or baking powder to create a reaction; treat this cocoa as you would standard Dutch-processed cocoa, replacing the *baking soda* with twice as much *baking powder* and leaving all other ingredient amounts the same. ∎

Extra Spicy Ginger Molasses Cookies

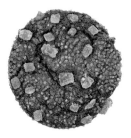

2⅓ cups (290g) unbleached
  all-purpose flour

2 teaspoons (12g) baking soda

½ teaspoon (1.5g) Diamond
  Crystal kosher salt

2 tablespoons (11g) natural cocoa powder

1 tablespoon (9g) ground ginger

2 teaspoons (8g) ground cinnamon

½ teaspoon (2g) ground black pepper

¼ teaspoon (1g) ground cloves

4 ounces (113g) unsalted butter,
  cut into ½-inch cubes

1 tablespoon (14g) unrefined
  extra-virgin coconut oil

1 cup packed + 3 tablespoons
  (253g) light-brown sugar

2 large eggs (100g), beaten

2 teaspoons (10g) vanilla extract

⅓ cup (113g) unsulfured molasses

½ cup (100g) finely chopped
  candied ginger

Demerara or sparkling sugar,
  to roll the cookies in

There is nothing quite like a soft, chewy, spicy ginger-molasses cookie. I designed this version to deliver the maximum amounts of each of those attributes. I chose light-brown sugar to encourage the dough to spread out while baking, and added a small amount of cocoa for depth of flavor, creating a deep and slightly savory base for the heaping amounts of spice to mingle with. This recipe makes a larger batch of smaller cookies than the others in the book; since it's a holiday cookie, I figured that would be helpful. ▶

◀ Whisk together the flour, baking soda, salt, cocoa powder, and spices in a medium bowl. Melt the butter with the coconut oil in a small saucepan over medium heat. Once it's melted, remove the butter from the heat and pour it into a large heatproof mixing bowl. Add the sugar, eggs, vanilla, and molasses to the butter, and beat the mixture with a whisk for about 1 minute to bring everything together.

◀ Add the dry ingredients and chopped candied ginger, and mix just until no bits of flour remain and you have a thick and sticky dough.

◀ Preheat your oven to 375°F (190°C). Line two half sheet pans with parchment paper.

◀ Use a spoon to portion the dough into thirty-six balls, transfer them to a plate or quarter sheet pan, and freeze them for 30 minutes. Transfer some demerara sugar to a small bowl. After 30 minutes, roll the balls of dough in the sugar, and place them on the prepared sheet pans, eighteen dough balls to a sheet. Bake them for 8 minutes, rotate the pans, and bake for an additional 7 to 8 minutes, until the cookies are puffy and set at the edges. The centers will look slightly damp, and the tops will be crackled like dry earth but when lightly touched on top will have a subtle puffy, squishy give. As the cookies cool, they will settle and firm up, and crackle more. Cool them for 15 to 20 minutes before eating. Store any uneaten cookies in a sealed container in the fridge. For the best results, warm them for 15 seconds in the microwave to refresh them before eating.

If you read "Dutch-Processed vs. Natural Cocoa" (page 34), you might be asking yourself why this ingredient list calls for natural cocoa. The secret agent is the molasses, which has an acidic pH and thus does the lifting for the recipe by neutralizing the baking soda and creating bubbles of air that aid in creating the texture of the cookie. ∎

2⅓ cups (290g) unbleached
   all-purpose flour

1 teaspoon (4g) baking powder

½ cup (100g) granulated sugar,
   + more for rolling the cookies

⅓ cup (38g) sifted confectioners' sugar,
   + more for rolling the cookies

½ teaspoon (1.5g) Diamond
   Crystal kosher salt

7 ounces (198g) cold unsalted
   butter, cubed

1 tablespoon (14g) unrefined
   extra-virgin coconut oil

2 large eggs (100g)

2 teaspoons (10g) vanilla extract

¼ cup (50g) rainbow sprinkles

I t might sound crazy to people who don't bake for a living, but professional bakers and pastry chefs can often read a recipe and picture the outcome without making it, sort of like a musician reading sheet music. When I decided to make a crinkle-style cookie, without the chocolate, I had a very specific toothsome texture in mind. I read many trusted bakers' versions of the basic crinkle and found the through-line that would create that lightly crisp, crackly exterior and squidgy cakelike interior. One of the major secrets to that? The coconut oil—do not skip it! It adds texture after the cookies have completely cooled, and a subtle flavor of grocery-store cake. I was VERY pleased with myself when I cracked the recipe after just two tries. ▶

◀ In the bowl of a stand mixer fitted with the paddle attachment, mix the flour, baking powder, sugars, and salt together, to disperse the powder and break up any lumps of sugar. Add the cold butter and coconut oil, and mix on low speed until the mixture resembles rustic sand, about 4 minutes.

◀ Add the eggs, vanilla, and sprinkles. Mix on low speed until the eggs have been completely incorporated and you have a thick dough.

◀ Preheat your oven to 375°F (190°C). Line two half sheet pans with parchment paper.

◀ Use a spoon to portion the dough into twelve balls, and roll them in granulated sugar, then in confectioners' sugar. Transfer them to a plate or quarter sheet pan, and freeze them for 30 minutes. Once they're chilled, roll each ball in confectioners' sugar once more.

◀ Place the balls of dough on the parchment-lined sheet pans, six well-spaced cookies on each sheet. Bake them for 10 minutes on the two center racks of your oven, rotate the pans, and bake for an additional 5 to 6 minutes, until the cookies are puffy and set at the edges. The centers will look cooked but when lightly touched on top will have a subtle puffy, squishy give. Eat them fresh, just after cooling. Store any uneaten cookies in a sealed container in the fridge. For the best results, warm them for 15 seconds in the microwave to refresh them before eating.

Vanilla Sprinkle Crinkle Cookies

Vegan Lemon Lavender Cookies

½ cup (100g) granulated sugar,
+ more for rolling the cookies

¼ cup packed (53g) light-brown sugar

2 teaspoons (2g) dried culinary lavender

2 teaspoons (4g) grated lemon zest

1½ cups (187g) unbleached
all-purpose flour

½ teaspoon (2g) baking powder

½ teaspoon (1.5g) Diamond
Crystal kosher salt

4 ounces (113g) cold unsalted
vegan butter

2 tablespoons (28g) lemon juice

2 tablespoons (20g) Bob's Red
Mill egg replacer mixed with
4 tablespoons cold water

1 teaspoon (5g) vanilla extract

This is another classic Fat + Flour cookie, which we converted to vegan during a nationwide egg shortage due to the bird flu of 2022 that caused the prices of eggs to triple overnight. Unexpectedly, this flavor has become a much-loved favorite by my customers. The combination of lemon and lavender can edge on soapy, so to make sure this flavor comes through as floral and fruity in a delicious way, we only use lavender flowers, never essential oil. ▶

◀ Before you begin mixing the cookie dough, put the sugars, lavender, and lemon zest into a bowl and rub them together with your fingers. This process warms the essential oils, to coax a more potent flavor out of the lavender and lemon zest.

◀ In the bowl of a stand mixer fitted with the paddle attachment, mix the flour, baking powder, lavender-lemon sugar, and salt together, to disperse the powder and break up any lumps of sugar. Add the cold butter, and mix on low speed until the mixture resembles rustic sand, about 4 minutes.

◀ Whisk the lemon juice and the hydrated egg replacer together, and add this to the buttery mixture along with the vanilla. Mix on low speed just until all the wet ingredients have been incorporated; then turn the speed to medium to bring the dough together.

◀ Use a spoon to portion the dough into twelve balls, and roll them in granulated sugar. Transfer them to a plate or quarter sheet pan, and freeze them for 30 minutes. Preheat your oven to 375°F (190°C). Line two half sheet pans with parchment paper.

◀ After 30 minutes, place the balls of dough on the two parchment-lined sheet pans, six well-spaced cookies on each sheet. Bake them for 10 minutes on the two center racks of your oven, rotate the pans, and bake for an additional 5 to 6 minutes, until the cookies are lightly browned at the edges and set but damp-looking in the center. Remove the cookies from the oven, and let them cool for a few minutes before eating them. Store any uneaten cookies in a sealed container in the fridge. For the best results, warm them for 15 seconds in the microwave to refresh them before eating.

For the Glaze

4 cups (460g) sifted confectioners' sugar

3 tablespoons (24g) meringue powder

6 tablespoons (88ml) warm water

Food coloring (optional)

For the Cookie Dough

8 ounces (226g) cold unsalted
    butter, cubed

¾ cup (150g) extra-fine granulated sugar

2½ cups (312g) unbleached
    all-purpose flour

½ teaspoon (1.5g) Diamond
    Crystal kosher salt

2 large egg yolks (28g)

2 teaspoons (10g) vanilla extract

I typically don't get excited when I see a pile of decorated holiday sugar cookies, because they usually taste like glazed cardboard, but of course THESE holiday sugar cookies taste amazing. Tender and buttery, with just enough salt to balance whatever frosting or glaze you choose to decorate them, they are delicious. At the bakery, we usually make them for Valentine's Day, Halloween, and Christmas. We always try to have as much fun as possible decorating, because that's the best part about a Shortbread Holiday Cookie, if you ask me. One of the ways we keep things fun is by stressing out LESS. We use meringue powder to make sure that our icing always comes out perfect. Meringue powder, which can be found in specialty food stores and online, is a mixture of dehydrated pasteurized egg whites, sugar, and sometimes starch. It's more reliable than fresh egg whites, since they often vary in size based on the time of year. ▶

◀ **Make the glaze** Combine the confectioners' sugar and meringue powder in the bowl of a stand mixer fitted with the paddle attachment.

◀ With the mixer running on low speed, slowly add the warm water, 1 tablespoon at a time, until you have a smooth mixture. Increase the speed to medium, and beat the glaze for 5 minutes, periodically scraping the sides of the mixing bowl with a rubber spatula to incorporate any dry sugar sticking to the bowl.

◀ Immediately transfer the glaze to a container with an airtight lid, to prevent a crust from forming on the surface. Store it in the container for up to 2 weeks in the fridge, or until you are ready to glaze the cookies.

◀ **Make the cookies** In a stand mixer fitted with the paddle attachment, mix the butter, sugar, flour, and salt on low speed until the mixture resembles rustic sand in texture, about 4 minutes. Whisk together the egg yolks and vanilla in a small bowl, and add this to the butter mixture. Mix on low speed until the eggs have been completely incorporated, but only until a dough forms. Turn the dough out onto a lightly floured counter, and knead it a few times to bring it together into a cohesive mass.

◀ Divide the dough into equal halves, and shape each into a flat disc, approximately 6 inches wide. Wrap each disc in plastic wrap or place into a separate zip-top bag. Refrigerate them for about an hour, until the dough feels cool and firm.

◀ Preheat your oven to 375°F (190°C). Line two half sheet pans with parchment paper.

◀ After the dough has chilled, remove the plastic wrap and roll the dough to ⅛ inch thick; this is best done between two pieces of lightly floured parchment paper. Use a cookie cutter to cut the dough into desired

Shortbread Holiday Cookies continues

Shortbread Holiday Cookies

shapes, and place the cookies 2 inches apart on the parchment-lined sheet pans. Refrigerate the cut cookies for 15 minutes. Bake them for 8 to 10 minutes on the two center racks of your oven, rotate the pans, and bake for an additional 5 to 6 minutes, until the cookies are lightly golden at the edges. Let them cool completely on the baking sheets.

◂ Glaze the cookies once they have completely cooled. Transfer the glaze to a small bowl that is larger than your cookie, and tint it with food coloring as desired. Hold a cookie by the edges, and dip it facedown into the glaze, being sure all of the surface touches the glaze. Pull the cookie straight up and out of the glaze, and allow the excess glaze to drip into the bowl. Gently shake the cookie back and forth to encourage the extra glaze to drip off the surface.

◂ Place a wire cooling rack over the previously used parchment-lined sheet pans. Place the glazed cookies on the cooling racks, glaze side up, allowing any excess to drip off the sides and onto the parchment paper below.

◂ Repeat with the remaining cookies. Allow them to dry, uncovered, for 1 hour, until the glaze has hardened. Store the finished cookies in a sealed container at room temperature.

Pecan Wedding Cookies (Mexican Polvorones)

MAKES 36 COOKIES

1½ cups (171g) roughly chopped pecans, toasted

¾ cup (86g) sifted confectioners' sugar, + more to roll the cookies in

2 cups (250g) unbleached all-purpose flour

½ teaspoon (1.5g) Diamond Crystal kosher salt

½ teaspoon (4g) ground cinnamon

6 ounces (170g) cold unsalted butter, cubed

3 tablespoons (42g) unrefined extra-virgin coconut oil

Only one of my grandmothers, Camille Rodriguez, was a good cook. The other, Isabel Mournian, was a salty, snappy "OK" cook, and she knew it. This was actually one of the most fun parts of going to her house: we never knew what she would serve us to eat, and some of her cooking misadventures provided my siblings and me with a lot to laugh about. She hated cooking, it seemed; she knew she wasn't great at it, and she had no plans of working to become better. One thing she did make well was Mexican Polvorones, and although her recipe would have been made with lard, I updated the cookies a little for modern times. They are no less buttery and tender, and their tiny size makes them very easy to eat. ▶

◀ Preheat your oven to 375°F (190°C). Line two half sheet pans with parchment paper.

◀ Blitz the toasted pecans in a food processor until they're finely ground, and place them in the bowl of a stand mixer fitted with the paddle attachment. Add the confectioners' sugar, flour, salt, and cinnamon, and mix on low speed for a few seconds to distribute everything. Add the butter and coconut oil, and mix on low speed until a cohesive dough forms.

◀ Use a spoon to portion the dough into thirty-six tablespoon-sized pieces, and place them on the parchment-lined baking sheets, about 1 inch apart, eighteen to a sheet. Bake them for 8 to 10 minutes on the two center racks of your oven, rotate the trays, and bake for an additional 5 to 6 minutes, until the cookies are lightly golden at the edges. Then let them cool completely before rolling them in confectioners' sugar. These cookies store well in an airtight container, but some of the confectioners' sugar might get absorbed into the cookies over time. Simply dust them again before serving to get that iconic Mexican Polvorones look. DO NOT breathe in when eating one of these cookies though, you will end up coughing if you do.

Vegan Crunchy-Chewy Peanut Butter Cookies

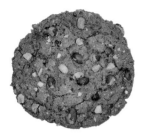

1½ cups (187g) unbleached
    all-purpose flour

1½ teaspoons (9g) baking soda

1 teaspoon (4g) baking powder

¾ cup (150g) granulated sugar,
    + more for topping the dough
    balls before baking

½ cup packed (100g) dark-brown sugar

1 teaspoon (3g) Diamond
    Crystal kosher salt

5½ ounces (158g) cold
    unsalted vegan butter

2 tablespoons (28g) nondairy milk

2 tablespoons (20g) Bob's Red
    Mill egg replacer mixed with
    4 tablespoons cold water

2 teaspoons (10g) vanilla extract

⅓ cup (90g) smooth peanut butter

1 cup (142g) roughly chopped
    peanuts, toasted

I have always had trouble with peanut-butter cookies; most of them seem to veer into a shortbread texture and get a little dry for me. I wanted a crispy but chewy peanut-butter cookie, one that had some bend and wasn't too crumbly. At the bakery, we figured out that the best way to get that ideal balance of textures was to make the cookie vegan, because vegan fats tend to keep cookies and cakes moist and chewy for longer than dairy-based butter. This cookie would not be half as good without the F+F baker Molly Donnellon, who went through countless trials to get this JUST right. ▶

◀ In the bowl of a stand mixer fitted with the paddle attachment, mix the flour, baking soda, baking powder, sugars, and salt together, to disperse the soda and powder and break up any lumps of sugar. Add the cold butter, and mix on low speed until the mixture resembles rustic sand, about 4 minutes.

◀ Whisk the milk, hydrated egg replacer, and vanilla together in a small bowl, and add this to the buttery mixture along with the peanut butter. Mix on low speed. Once all the wet ingredients have been incorporated, turn the speed to medium to bring the dough together.

◀ Transfer the chopped peanuts and the extra granulated sugar to two small bowls. Use a spoon to portion the dough into twelve balls, and roll them all in sugar and then in the chopped peanuts. Transfer them to a plate or quarter sheet pan, and freeze them for 30 minutes.

◀ Preheat your oven to 375°F (190°C). Line two half sheet pans with parchment paper. After 30 minutes, place the balls of dough on the parchment-lined pans, six well-spaced cookies on each. Bake them for 10 minutes on the two center racks of your oven, rotate the pans, and bake for an additional 5 to 6 minutes, until the cookies are lightly browned at the edges and set but damp-looking in the center. Remove the cookies from the oven, and cool them for 15 to 20 minutes before eating. Store any uneaten cookies in a sealed container in the fridge. For the best results, warm them for 15 seconds in the microwave to refresh them before eating.

For the Cookies

1 cup (142g) roughly chopped peanuts, toasted

½ cup (100g) granulated sugar

1 batch Vegan Crunchy-Chewy Peanut Butter Cookie dough (page 46)

For the Peanut Butter Filling

4 ounces (113g) soft unsalted vegan butter

3 tablespoons (45g) room-temperature smooth peanut butter

1 cup (115g) sifted confectioners' sugar

¼ cup (28g) cornstarch

Pinch of Diamond Crystal kosher salt

O K, this recipe does involve creaming, but I promise, it's worth it. You do need to cream butter in order to make the filling for these incredibly addictive Nutter Butter knockoff cookies.

It's not a Nutter Butter—it's better. If you grew up enjoying those crunchy, nutty sandwich cookies, you will love this version. They are chewy and tender, and they have plenty of peanut flavor throughout. You can adjust the size of the cookies, to make smaller, cuter cookie sandwiches; if so, you will need to adjust the baking time by a few minutes. ▶

◀ **Make the cookies** Transfer the chopped peanuts and the granulated sugar to two small bowls. Use a spoon to portion the dough into twenty-four balls, and roll them all in sugar and then in the chopped peanuts. Transfer them to a plate or quarter sheet pan, and freeze them for 30 minutes.

◀ Preheat your oven to 375°F (190°C). Line two half sheet pans with parchment paper. After 30 minutes, place the balls of dough on the parchment-lined baking sheets, twelve well-spaced cookies on each sheet. Bake them for 10 minutes on the two center racks of your oven, rotate the pans, and bake for an additional 5 to 6 minutes, until the cookies are lightly browned at the edges and set but damp-looking in the center. Remove the cookies from the oven, and let them cool completely to room temperature.

◀ **Make the peanut-butter filling** In the bowl of a stand mixer fitted with the paddle attachment, mix the butter and peanut butter on low speed until the mixture is creamy and all the butter is emulsified with the peanut butter, about 4 minutes. Add the confectioners' sugar, cornstarch, and salt to the bowl. Drape a kitchen towel over the mixer, and mix the filling on low speed until the dry ingredients have been incorporated into the butter mixture. Increase the speed to medium, and mix until the mixture is slightly aerated and fluffy-looking—about 2 minutes.

◀ Line up the cookies into pairs, turning one of each pair over. Scoop a tablespoon of filling onto the upside-down cookies, and place another cookie on top to create a sandwich. Gently press down to secure the filling. These cookies keep well in an airtight container, in a cool place.

Vegan PB Sandwich Cookies

Brownies
and Bars

If a chocolate-chip cookie is the perfect gauge of a baker's personality, I'd say a brownie has got to be a glimpse into their soul.

Everyone has their preferred "cut" of the brownie. I like an edge piece, but a corner has a bit too much texture for me. What about you—do you reach only for the center of the pan? A well-made bar has so many opportunities to please whatever type of brownie lover you are. Do you give the side eye to anything without a walnut? Maybe you're not into dark chocolate at all, and what you are really looking for is a buttery, chewy, brown-sugar dough baked in a dish with nuts and maybe some white chocolate. I have thought of all you sweets lovers in this chapter—something for everyone.

Let's get something out of the way first: a brownie is a cake. I have lost sleep and argued for hours with other bakers and ended up back here: a brownie is definitely a cake. The original brownie recipe was in fact written to be a tiny tea cake to be given to guests of the Palmer Hotel in Chicago, Illinois, in 1898.

However you choose to categorize them, in my opinion the best brownies are made by creating an emulsion of fat, chocolate, sugar, and eggs. I once would have said that the ideal "brownie" used both melted chocolate and cocoa powder . . . that is, until I started making "brownies" with white chocolate and ventured into a whole new territory of this bar cake that I am calling a brownie, though I don't know what

it actually is—it's more like a "beigey," but that doesn't sound as good.

Whatever you decide to call it, I prefer to mix brownies with what's called the emulsion method because I enjoy the sugary, papery top that it creates. This is a result of the furious mixing, which breaks down the sugar a little bit and imparts some air, which rises to the surface during baking and leaves behind that shiny crackled top. If this book had been written in the 1990s, the author would have put in a little joke here about the beating process being the arm workout that makes it OK to eat a brownie or two, but, fortunately, I know better. The truth is, it's pretty much always "OK" to eat a brownie, especially if you've made it from scratch.

Sitting alongside the "brownies" (cakes) in this chapter are a few true bar "cookies," like Lemon, Browned Butter, and Rosemary Bars (page 66) and Buttery Date and Coconut Bars (page 72). All of these feature a press-in crust, made by creating a sort of streusely dough and pressing it into a parchment-lined pan. Sometimes you press half the crust into the bottom and save the rest to use as a crumble for the top. Shortbread is the most classic of these press-in bakes, as in the Fig Leaf and Vanilla Shortbread (page 70).

Whatever type of bar I am making, I always remove the bars from the pan before cutting into them. I find that, once they've cooled, they are easy to remove by lifting the paper at the sides and sliding them onto a cutting board, where you can cut perfect squares, rectangles, or triangles with ease. This also saves the pan from getting cut lines, which can give things like lemon bars a metallic taste.

Bar bakes, like brownies and their nonchocolatey cousins, are a great way to make a lot of servings at once. If I am going to a holiday party, I can bake one tray of something and cut that into whatever size treat meets my needs. That's the beauty of a bar, one of the workhorses of the dessert world, and damn delicious, too! ∎

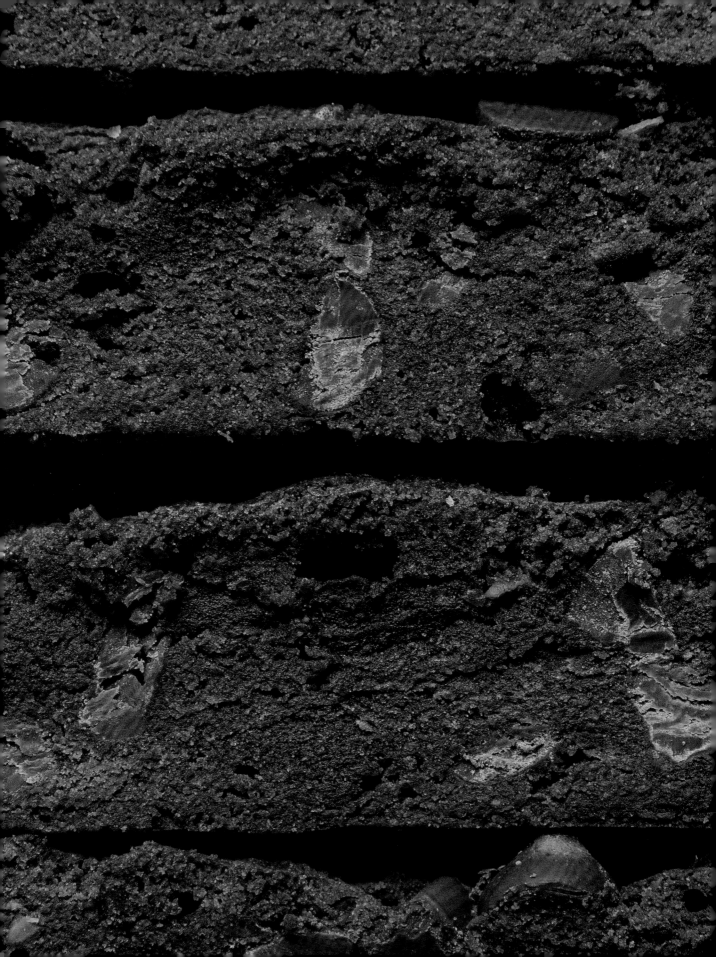

Dark Chocolate Brownies

8 ounces (226g) unsalted butter

1⅓ cups (226g) roughly
chopped 72% chocolate

3 tablespoons (42g) roughly chopped
Baker's unsweetened chocolate

⅔ cup packed (142g) dark-brown sugar

1½ cups (300g) granulated sugar

1½ teaspoons (4.5g) Diamond
Crystal kosher salt

4 large eggs (200g)

1 large egg yolk (14g)

2 teaspoons (10g) vanilla extract

1⅓ cups (208g) unbleached bread flour

½ cup (42g) natural cocoa powder

1¼ cups (250g) milk-chocolate chips

T he Dark Chocolate Brownie is the standard that all brownies are measured against. In my opinion, this recipe is perfect just as it is. It doesn't need nuts, or flaky sea salt, or anything other than what is in the list of ingredients. That's not to say you can't dress these gals up with some fun add-ins. Toasted pecans or walnuts are great additions, chopped-up halva candy and a sprinkling of sesame seeds are another lovely choice—just know that you are gilding the lily. ▶

◀ Preheat your oven to 375°F (190°C). Lightly grease a 9-by-13-by-1-inch quarter sheet pan, and line the bottom and sides with parchment paper.

◀ Put the butter into a small saucepan, and heat it over medium heat. Stir every few minutes and watch it closely to prevent it from browning. While the butter is melting, put the 72% and Baker's chocolate into a heatproof bowl. When the butter is melted, pour it over the chocolate, and stir gently until every piece of chocolate has melted into the butter.

◀ In a large mixing bowl, combine the dark-brown sugar, granulated sugar, salt, eggs, egg yolk, and vanilla. Use a hand mixer to whisk vigorously for 1 minute, until the mixture is pale in color and very creamy-looking. It is important to beat the eggs and sugar really well, because this is how you get a shiny, flaky top layer on your brownie. Add the melted chocolate and butter to the egg mixture, and whisk until everything is combined. Add the flour and cocoa powder, and use a spatula to incorporate them, mixing just until no dry bits of flour remain.

◀ Transfer the batter to the prepared pan, and smooth the surface. Gently rap the pan on the counter to burst any air pockets in the batter. Sprinkle the milk-chocolate chips onto the surface of the batter, and gently press them in just a little bit; some of them will sink during baking, and that's OK!

◀ Bake for 10 minutes on the center rack of your oven, rotate the pan, and continue baking until a cake tester or toothpick inserted in the center comes out with very moist crumbs still clinging to it, about 15 minutes longer. The edges will set and wrinkle a little, and the center will still appear unset. If you have beaten the egg mixture enough, the brownies will have a wonderful shiny surface.

◀ Remove the brownies from the oven, and allow them to cool in the pan. Eat them immediately, or, if you enjoy a chewier brownie, put the pan in the freezer and chill them for ½ hour. Cutting the brownies while they are very cold will produce a densely packed, chewy texture and clean cuts. Store them in an airtight container at room temperature for 1 week or in the fridge for 2 weeks.

8 ounces (226g) unsalted butter

1 tablespoon (6g) Earl Grey tea, pulverized

¾ cup (127g) roughly chopped white-chocolate

½ cup packed (106g) light-brown sugar

1 cup (200g) granulated sugar

¾ teaspoon (2g) Diamond Crystal kosher salt

4 large eggs (200g)

2 teaspoons (10g) vanilla extract

1⅔ cups (200g) unbleached bread flour

1¼ cups (212g) roughly chopped 72% chocolate

These are made with white chocolate—an uncommon move in brownie recipes, and I'm not sure why, because, wow, are they delicious. This recipe yields a cake that bakes into a variety of textures in one pan: chewy edge, extremely chewy corner, and fudgelike center. The brownie is the only cake that's allowed to have so much textural variety in one pan.

This bar is flavored with Earl Grey tea—steeped in the melting butter—along with vanilla and the creamy dairy flavor of white chocolate in place of traditional dark chocolate. The result of these elements commingling is a "brownie" that's aromatic and elegant, and very delicious.

If your first question is "Can I use a different tea?" or "Can I leave the tea out?" Yes, of course. ▶

◀ Preheat your oven to 375°F (190°C). Lightly grease a 9-by-13-by-1-inch quarter sheet pan, and line the bottom and sides with parchment paper.

◀ Put the butter and pulverized tea into a small saucepan, and heat the mixture over medium heat. Stir every few minutes and watch it closely to prevent it from browning. While the butter is melting, put the white chocolate into a heatproof bowl. When the butter is melted, pour it over the chocolate, and stir gently until every piece of white chocolate has melted into the butter.

◀ In a large mixing bowl, combine the light-brown sugar, granulated sugar, salt, eggs, and vanilla. Use a hand mixer to beat vigorously for 1 minute, until the mixture is pale in color and very creamy-looking. It is important to beat the eggs and sugar really well, because this is how you get a shiny, flaky top layer on your brownie. Add the melted chocolate and butter to the egg mixture, and whisk until everything is combined. Add the flour, and use a spatula to incorporate it, mixing just until no dry bits of flour remain.

◀ Transfer the batter to the prepared pan, and smooth the surface. Gently rap the pan on the counter to burst any air pockets in the batter. Scatter the chopped 72% chocolate over the top, and gently press it in a little (most will sink into the batter). Bake for 10 minutes on the center rack of your oven, rotate the pan, and continue baking until a cake tester or toothpick inserted in the center comes out with very moist crumbs still clinging to it, about 15 minutes longer. The edges will show some browning and wrinkling, and the center will still appear a bit unset. If you have beaten the egg mixture enough, there will be a wonderful shiny surface to the brownies.

◀ Remove the brownies from the oven, and allow them to cool in the pan. Eat immediately, or, if you enjoy a chewier brownie, put the pan in the freezer for ½ hour. Cutting the brownies while they are very cold will produce a densely packed, chewy texture and clean cuts. Store them in an airtight container at room temperature for 1 week or in the fridge for 2 weeks.

London Fog
Brownies

Abuelita Milk Chocolate Brownies

MAKES ONE 9 × 13 INCH TRAY OF BROWNIES

8 ounces (226g) unsalted butter

1 tablespoon (18g) pulverized masala chai, such as Søul Chai, or 2 teaspoons (8g) ground cinnamon

3 tablespoons (44ml) vinegar-based hot sauce, such as Zab's Datil Pepper Hot Sauce

1 cup (170g) milk chocolate, + 1¼ cups (212g) milk-chocolate chips to add to the batter before baking

½ cup packed (106g) light-brown sugar

¾ cup (150g) granulated sugar

1 teaspoon (3g) Diamond Crystal kosher salt

4 large eggs (200g)

2 teaspoons (10g) vanilla extract

1⅔ cups (208g) unbleached bread flour

½ cup (42g) natural cocoa powder

W hen I set out to create these Abuelita Brownies (named after the iconic Mexican Hot Chocolate brand that became popular in the 1990s), I added some pulverized chai tea in lieu of cinnamon, and various ground hot chilis for even more warmth. While working in the bakery kitchen one afternoon, I wanted to make a batch of these brownies for a friend, but I was missing all of my special ground chilis. I reached for a bottle of my favorite hot sauce—Zab's Datil Pepper Hot Sauce and measured a few glugs of it into the batter until it tasted right. This batch of brownies was so good that I changed the recipe to include Zab's or any other vinegar-based hot sauce, something I figure most home cooks would have on hand at all times. ▶

◀ Preheat your oven to 375°F (190°C). Lightly grease a 9-by-13-by-1-inch quarter sheet pan, and line the bottom and sides with parchment paper.

◀ Put the butter, pulverized chai, and hot sauce into a small saucepan, and heat the mixture over medium heat. Stir every few minutes and watch it closely to prevent it from browning. While the butter is melting, put 1 cup (170g) milk chocolate into a medium heatproof bowl. When the butter is melted, pour it over the chocolate, and stir gently until every piece of chocolate has melted into the butter.

◀ In a large mixing bowl, combine the light-brown sugar, granulated sugar, salt, eggs, and vanilla. Use a hand mixer to beat vigorously for 1 minute, until the mixture is pale in color and very creamy-looking. It is important to beat the eggs and sugar really well, because this is how you get a shiny, flaky top layer on your brownie. Add the melted chocolate and butter to the egg mixture, and whisk until everything is combined. Add the flour and cocoa powder, and use a spatula to incorporate them, mixing just until no dry bits of flour remain.

◀ Transfer the batter to the prepared pan, and smooth the surface. Gently rap the pan on the counter to burst any air pockets in the batter. Scatter the milk-chocolate chips over the top, and gently press them in a little (most will sink into the batter). Bake for 10 minutes on the center rack of your oven, rotate the pan, and continue baking until a cake tester or toothpick inserted in the center comes out with very moist crumbs still clinging to it, about 15 minutes longer. The edges will set and wrinkle a little, and the center will still appear a bit unset. If you have beaten the egg mixture enough, there will be a wonderful shiny surface to the brownies.

◀ Remove the brownies from the oven, and allow them to cool in the pan. Eat immediately, or, if you enjoy a chewier brownie, put the pan in the freezer and chill for ½ hour. Cutting the brownies while they are very cold will produce a densely packed, chewy texture and clean cuts. Store them in an airtight container at room temperature for 1 week or in the fridge for 2 weeks.

MAKES ONE 9 × 13 INCH TRAY OF BROWNIES

8 ounces (226g) unsalted butter

½ cup + 3 tablespoons (185g) smooth peanut butter

1 cup (170g) roughly chopped milk chocolate

½ cup packed (106g) dark-brown sugar

¾ cup (150g) granulated sugar

1 teaspoon (3g) Diamond Crystal kosher salt

4 large eggs (200g)

2 teaspoons (10g) vanilla extract

1⅔ cups (208g) unbleached all-purpose flour

½ cup (42g) natural cocoa powder

1 cup (170g) 72% chocolate chips

This is probably the most indulgent recipe I have ever made, but I couldn't stop myself from adding peanut butter to my milk-chocolate brownie base, because I really love the peanutty-chocolatey combo. You can use either a natural or a more processed peanut butter in this recipe, because, unlike that of a cookie, brownie texture is created more by the ratio of sugar, egg, and butter than by the type of peanut butter used. ▶

◀ Preheat your oven to 375°F (190°C). Lightly grease a 9-by-13-by-1-inch quarter sheet pan, and line the bottom and sides with parchment paper.

◀ Put the butter into a small saucepan, and heat it over medium heat. Stir every few minutes and watch it closely to prevent it from browning. While the butter is melting, put the peanut butter and milk chocolate into a heatproof bowl. When the butter is melted, pour it over the chocolate, and stir gently until every piece of chocolate has melted into the butter.

◀ In a large mixing bowl, combine the light-brown sugar, granulated sugar, salt, eggs, and vanilla. Use a hand mixer to beat vigorously for 1 minute, until the mixture is pale in color and very creamy-looking. It is important to beat the eggs and sugar really well, because this is how you get a shiny, flaky top layer on your brownie. Add the melted chocolate and butter to the egg mixture, and whisk until everything is combined. Add the flour and cocoa powder, and use a spatula to incorporate them, mixing just until no dry bits of flour remain.

◀ Transfer the batter to the prepared pan, and smooth the surface. Gently rap the pan on the counter to burst any air pockets in the batter. Scatter the 72% chocolate chips over the top, and gently press them in a little (most will sink into the batter). Bake for 10 minutes on the center rack of your oven, rotate the pan, and continue baking until a cake tester or toothpick inserted in the center comes out with very moist crumbs still clinging to it, about 15 minutes longer. The edges will set and wrinkle a little, and the center will still appear a bit unset. If you have beaten the egg mixture enough, there will be a wonderful shiny surface to the brownies.

◀ Remove the brownies from the oven, and allow them to cool in the pan. Eat immediately, or, if you enjoy a chewier brownie, put the pan in the freezer and chill for ½ hour. Cutting the brownies while they are very cold will produce a densely packed, chewy texture and clean cuts. Store them in an airtight container at room temperature for 1 week or in the fridge for 2 weeks.

Milk Chocolate and Peanut Butter Brownies

White Chocolate, Vanilla, and Coconut Brownies

8 ounces (226g) unsalted butter

¾ cup (127g) roughly chopped
white chocolate

½ cup packed (106g) light-brown sugar

¾ cup (150g) granulated sugar

1 teaspoon (3g) Diamond
Crystal kosher salt

¼ cup (36g) coconut-milk powder

3 large eggs (150g)

2 teaspoons (10g) vanilla extract

2 cups (240g) unbleached bread flour

1 cup (93g) unsweetened
shredded coconut

½ cup (85g) 72% chocolate chips

Ask anyone who works with me: I love coconut. Sue me, I think some well-placed coconut takes a buttery bake over the top to baked-good heaven. These brownies require a few tricks to get the most coconut into them without sacrificing texture, because that is the trap with coconut—too much and you will be chewing . . . forever. Coconut extract often tastes like sunscreen to me, so I avoid it. The flavor in this recipe comes from two levels of coconut infusion: powdered coconut milk (for creamy coconut flavor) and shredded coconut on top. ▶

◀ Preheat your oven to 375°F (190°C). Lightly grease a 9-by-13-by-1-inch quarter sheet pan, and line the bottom and sides with parchment paper.

◀ Melt the butter in a small saucepan, and heat it over medium heat. Transfer the white chocolate to a heatproof bowl. Pour the melted butter over the chocolate, and stir gently until every piece of white chocolate has melted into the butter.

◀ In a large mixing bowl, combine the light-brown sugar, granulated sugar, salt, coconut-milk powder, eggs, and vanilla. Use a hand mixer to beat vigorously for 1 minute, until the mixture is pale in color and very creamy-looking. It is important to beat the eggs and sugar really well, because this is how you get a shiny, flaky top layer on your brownie. Add the melted chocolate and butter to the egg mixture, and whisk until everything is combined. Add the flour and shredded coconut (reserving a small handful for topping the brownies later) to the bowl, and use a spatula to incorporate them, mixing just until no dry bits of flour remain.

◀ Transfer the batter to the prepared pan, and smooth the surface. Gently rap the pan on the counter to burst any air pockets in the batter. Scatter the reserved shredded coconut over the surface, and lightly press it into the batter. Sprinkle the 72% chocolate chips across the layer of coconut. Bake for 10 minutes on the center rack of your oven, rotate the pan, and continue baking until a cake tester or toothpick inserted in the center comes out with very moist crumbs still clinging to it, about 15 minutes longer. The edges will set and wrinkle a little, and the center will still appear a bit unset. If you have beaten the egg mixture enough, there will be a wonderful shiny surface to the brownies.

◀ Remove the brownies from the oven, and allow them to cool in the pan. Eat immediately, or, if you enjoy a chewier brownie, put the pan in the freezer and chill for ½ hour. Cutting the brownies while they are very cold will produce a densely packed, chewy texture and clean cuts. Store them in an airtight container at room temperature for 1 week or in the fridge for 2 weeks.

MAKES ONE 9 x 13 INCH TRAY OF BROWNIES

8 ounces (226g) unsalted butter

1⅓ cups (226g) roughly chopped 72% chocolate

3 tablespoons (42g) chopped unsweetened Baker's chocolate

⅔ cup + 1 tablespoon (155g) packed dark-brown sugar

1½ cups (300g) granulated sugar

1½ teaspoons (4.5g) Diamond Crystal kosher salt

4 large eggs (200g)

1 large egg yolk (14g)

2 teaspoons (10g) vanilla extract

1⅔ cups (208g) all-purpose gluten-free flour

¾ cup (63g) Dutch-processed cocoa powder

1 cup (114g) roughly chopped pecans, toasted

1½ cups (65g) mini marshmallows

12 large marshmallows (84g)

Brownies are one of the easiest bakes to make gluten-free because they typically use a lot less flour than most cakes and cookies. This GF brownie recipe has a secret gooey enhancing ingredient: the small marshmallows folded into the batter melt while baking, creating a wonderful mochi-like texture. The large marshmallows roast on the surface, creating a s'mores-like effect. Yes, you need both to achieve this perfect balance. ▶

◀ Preheat your oven to 375°F (190°C). Lightly grease a 9-by-13-by-1-inch quarter sheet pan, and line the bottom and sides with parchment paper.

◀ Put the butter into a small saucepan, and heat it over medium heat. Stir every few minutes and watch it closely to prevent it from browning. While the butter is melting, put both chocolates into a heatproof bowl. When the butter is melted, pour it over the chocolate, and stir gently until every piece of chocolate has melted into the butter.

◀ In a large mixing bowl, combine the dark-brown sugar, granulated sugar, salt, eggs, egg yolk, and vanilla. Use a hand mixer to beat vigorously for 1 minute, until the mixture is pale in color and very creamy-looking. It is important to beat the eggs and sugar really well, because this is how you get a shiny, flaky top layer on your brownie. Add the melted chocolate and butter to the egg mixture, and whisk until everything is combined. Whisk the flour and cocoa powder in a small bowl, and add them to the melted chocolate mixture along with the pecans and mini marshmallows, and use a spatula to incorporate them, mixing just until no dry bits of flour remain.

◀ Transfer the batter to the prepared pan, and smooth the surface. Gently rap the pan on the counter to burst any air pockets in the batter. Place the large marshmallows on the surface, and lightly press them into the batter. Bake for 10 minutes on the center rack of your oven, rotate the pan, and continue baking until a cake tester or toothpick inserted in the center comes out with very moist crumbs still clinging to it, about 15 minutes longer. The edges will set and wrinkle a little, the large marshmallows will be browned and starting to lose their shape, and the center will still appear a bit unset. If you have beaten the egg mixture enough, there will be a wonderful shiny surface to the brownies.

◀ Remove the brownies from the oven, and allow them to cool in the pan. Eat immediately, or, if you enjoy a chewier brownie, put the pan in the freezer and chill for ½ hour. Cutting the brownies while they are very cold will produce a densely packed, chewy texture and clean cuts. Store them in an airtight container at room temperature for 1 week or in the fridge for 2 weeks.

Marshmallow Pecan Brownies (GF)

Lemon, Browned Butter, and Rosemary Bars

MAKES ONE 9 × 13 INCH TRAY

For the Shortbread Crust

8 ounces (226g) unsalted butter

1 teaspoon (2g) finely chopped
fresh rosemary

2½ cups + 1 tablespoon (320g)
unbleached all-purpose flour

5 tablespoons (50g) cornstarch

¾ cup (86g) sifted confectioners'
sugar, + more for dusting the bars

1 teaspoon (3g) Diamond
Crystal kosher salt

For the Lemon Filling

2½ ounces (71g) unsalted butter

½ cup (62g) unbleached all-purpose flour

2 cups (400g) granulated sugar

1 teaspoon (3g) Diamond
Crystal kosher salt

4 large eggs (200g)

6 large egg yolks (14g)

1 tablespoon (6g) grated lemon zest

When I got started on this recipe, I hadn't made lemon bars in over 10 years. Not because I don't like them (I love them), but because it is very hard to improve on a perfect recipe. Most bakeries I have worked in bake lemon bars directly from the first Tartine Bakery book, a magnificent recipe by Liz Prueitt. With that holy-grail recipe in mind, I decided to look back to when I was baking these bars a lot—the late 1990s, the early 2000s—for inspiration. I decided to add just a little rosemary, and brown the butter for the crust—both nods to the popular flavors of that period of time. For the filling, I looked to the brilliant mind of Stella Parks, whose Sunny Lemon Bars recipe calls for pre-cooking the filling to guarantee a silky, set curd. Using that technique, I reworked my lemon-chess-pie filling, which calls for melted butter, making it a true curd, something I was shocked to find missing from most lemon-bar fillings. What I ended up with is a mouth-puckering, unctuous, savory, and sweet lemon bar. What more can you ask for from a recipe? ▶

◀ Preheat your oven to 375°F (190°C). Lightly grease a 9-by-13-by-1-inch quarter sheet pan, and line the bottom and sides with parchment paper; this pan is for baking the lemon bars. Line a second quarter sheet pan with parchment paper covering only the bottom; this pan is for baking the crumble topping.

◀ **Make the shortbread crust** Melt the butter in a small saucepan over medium heat, and continue cooking until it's browned, scraping the bottom of the pot frequently. While the butter is still hot, add the chopped rosemary. It will sputter a little, but stir it in; pour the hot browned butter and all the browned bits into a heatproof bowl to cool completely.

◄ In the bowl of a stand mixer fitted with the paddle attachment, combine the flour, cornstarch, confectioners' sugar, and salt, and mix on low speed until the mixture resembles a crumble, about 5 to 7 minutes. Remove roughly two-thirds of the crumble for the crust, and lightly press it into the fully lined sheet pan, getting it edge to edge on all sides. Bake the pressed crust for 20 to 25 minutes, until the edges are just beginning to become golden and the center is very lightly browned and opaque. Sprinkle the rest of the crumble on the other prepared pan and bake until it's lightly golden brown, about 15 minutes.

◄ **While the shortbread crust is baking, make the lemon filling** Melt the butter in a small saucepan over medium heat. Transfer the melted butter to a small heatproof bowl; keep the saucepan handy for later use. Whisk the flour, sugar, and salt together in a medium bowl. Add the melted butter along with the eggs, egg yolks, and lemon zest. Whisk to combine everything. Transfer the mixture to the saucepan, and cook over medium heat until it thickens into a curd and the temperature registers 170°F on an instant-read thermometer, 7 to 10 minutes.

◄ Once the curd is thickened, pour it through a fine-mesh strainer into a heatproof bowl. Pour the curd over the baked shortbread crust when the crust is fresh out of the oven, and use an offset spatula to smooth the surface. Reduce the oven temp to 350°F (176°C). Return the pan to the oven for an additional 10 to 15 minutes, until the surface of the bars is set but still has a slight jiggle in the center. While the lemon bars are hot, scatter the baked crumbs over the surface. Allow the bars to cool for 2 hours; then refrigerate for at least 2 hours more, or overnight for best results. Remove the lemon bars from the pan before cutting them, using the paper to lift them out. Slice and dust them liberally with confectioners' sugar. Store leftovers in the fridge, in a sealed container, and enjoy them cold.

Pecan Honey Caramel Bars

MAKES ONE **9 × 13** INCH TRAY

For the Shortbread Crust

8 ounces (226g) unsalted butter, melted and cooled to room temperature

2½ cups (312g) unbleached all-purpose flour

½ cup (80g) cornstarch

¾ cup (86g) sifted confectioners' sugar

½ teaspoon (2g) baking powder

1 teaspoon (3g) Diamond Crystal kosher salt

For the Pecan Honey Caramel Filling

8 ounces (226g) unsalted butter

½ cup (168g) honey, preferably wildflower

¼ cup packed (53g) dark-brown sugar

1 teaspoon (3g) Diamond Crystal kosher salt

1 tablespoon (7g) freeze-dried chicory powder or espresso powder

1 tablespoon (5g) vanilla extract

2 large eggs (100g)

2 large egg yolks (28g)

2 cups (228g) roughly chopped pecans, toasted

1 cup (170g) 72% chocolate chips

These delicious, just-sweet-enough bars are almost pecan pie in bar form, but with a lower goo factor. I love them cut into cute petite squares and alongside a nice coffee—a perfect beginning-of-fall treat! I've used chicory in the filling to give a bitter, noncaffeinated edge, but espresso powder will do just as well. Make sure those pecans are nicely toasted so they retain some of that buttery crunch in the filling. ▶

◀ Preheat your oven to 375°F (190°C). Lightly grease a 9-by-13-by-1-inch quarter sheet pan, and line the bottom and sides with parchment paper.

◀ **Make the shortbread crust** In the bowl of a stand mixer fitted with the paddle attachment, combine all the ingredients and mix on low speed until the mixture resembles a crumble, about 5 to 7 minutes. Press the crumble into the prepared pan, getting it edge to edge on all sides. Use an offset spatula to smooth the surface. Bake the pressed crust for 20 to 25 minutes, until the edges are just beginning to become golden and the center is very lightly browned and opaque.

◀ **While the shortbread crust is baking, make the pecan-honey-caramel filling** Melt the butter in a small saucepan over medium heat. Add the honey, brown sugar, and salt, bring the mixture to a rolling boil over medium heat, and let it boil for 2 minutes. Remove the pot from the heat, and transfer the honey caramel to a heatproof bowl. Let it cool for a few minutes. Mix the chicory powder with 2 tablespoons water in a small bowl, and add it to the caramel, along with the vanilla. Add the eggs and egg yolks, and whisk until the mixture is glossy and smooth. Add the pecans, and set the mixture aside until you're ready to use it.

◄ When the crust is finished baking, remove it from the oven and set it on a heatproof surface. Add the chocolate chips to the honey mixture, and stir them in. Pour the filling on top of the crust, and use a spatula to settle the surface, moving the nuts and chocolate around so they are evenly distributed. Reduce the oven temp to 350°F (176°C). Return the bars to the oven, and bake for 10 minutes, until the filling is slightly puffed at the edges and the center is set.

◄ Allow the bars to cool at room temperature for 2 hours before cutting. Store leftovers in the fridge in a sealed container, and either enjoy them cold or temper them for a few minutes before diving in.

Fig Leaf and Vanilla Shortbread

MAKES ONE 9 × 13 INCH TRAY OF SHORTBREAD

For the Fig-Leaf-and-Vanilla Sugar

¼ cup (50g) granulated sugar

¼ teaspoon (2g) ground vanilla bean

2 teaspoons (10g) ground toasted fig leaves (see Note, page 71)

For the Shortbread

8 ounces (226g) cold unsalted butter

2½ cups (312g) unbleached all-purpose flour

¾ cup (86g) sifted confectioners' sugar

1 teaspoon (3g) Diamond Crystal kosher salt

1 large egg white (33g) + pinch of salt

1 teaspoon (5g) cold water

Right before Labor Day, the figs on our trees begin to ripen quickly, and a fight begins to get a perfect ripe fig before a bird eats a third of it and leaves a rotting carcass on the branch. I decided that, if the birds were going to get LITERALLY ALL MY RIPE FIGS, then at least I could salvage some of the season by using the leaves, like I had seen some of my favorite pastry chefs do. One afternoon, I toasted a few leaves for just a few minutes in a toaster oven and ground them with a mortar and pestle. The smell of the earthy green powder was delightful, sort of like vanilla but also a bit like coconut. The first thing I used them in was this shortbread. My husband brought it to work, and a coworker pronounced it the best shortbread he'd ever had in his life. Hard to beat that kind of praise! ▶

◀ Preheat your oven to 350°F (176°C). Lightly grease a 9-by-13-by-1-inch quarter sheet pan, and line the bottom and sides with parchment paper.

◀ **Make the fig-leaf-and-vanilla sugar** Whisk the granulated sugar, vanilla bean, and fig leaf together in a small bowl. Put 1 tablespoon of this into the prepared pan, and rotate the pan to coat the greased paper with sugar. If you don't need a full tablespoon to cover all the paper, return what you don't need to the rest of the fig-leaf sugar for later use.

◀ **Make the shortbread** In the bowl of a stand mixer fitted with the paddle attachment, mix the cold butter, flour, confectioners' sugar, and salt on low speed until the mixture resembles a smooth and pasty dough, about 5 to 7 minutes. Press the dough into the prepared pan, and use an offset spatula to smooth the surface.

◀ Whisk the egg white and water together until the mixture is foamy and the egg white is loose and liquid. Use a pastry brush to coat the surface of the shortbread with the egg white, just until covered. Discard any remaining egg white. Sprinkle the rest of the fig-leaf sugar on top of the shortbread, and rotate the pan a few times to coat the surface evenly. Use a fork to dock holes all over the shortbread (you can be decorative about this and do a design of your choosing!).

◀ Bake it for 40 to 50 minutes, until the surface of the shortbread is golden brown. Allow the shortbread to cool for 1 hour before slicing it. Store it at room temperature in a sealed container.

Processing fig leaves for baking is pretty simple. Preheat your oven to 200°F (93°C). Pick and wash the younger fig leaves, then lay them in a single layer on a baking sheet. Bake them until they are dry and crisp but still green, 20 to 30 minutes. Remove the fibrous stems from the dried leaves, and discard them. Crush the leaves with your fingers, then grind them to a fine powder, using a mortar and pestle or a spice grinder. Store the ground fig leaves in a sealed container; a jar with a tight-fitting lid is best for that. ∎

Buttery Date and Coconut Bars

MAKES ONE **9 × 13** INCH TRAY

For the Coconut-Oat Crumble Crust

1 cup (226g) cold unsalted butter, cut into 1-inch cubes, + more for greasing the pan

1½ cups (135g) rolled oats

1¾ cups (218g) unbleached all-purpose flour

½ cup (46g) unsweetened shredded coconut

1 teaspoon (6g) baking soda

1 cup packed (213g) brown sugar

For the Date Filling

1 cup (236ml) hot brewed coffee

2 cups (300g) chopped medjool dates

1 teaspoon (3g) Diamond Crystal kosher salt

These bars are packed with natural sweetness and a caramel note from the dates. They are sort of a perfect bar to snack on at 3:00 p.m., when you need a boost of energy; reminiscent of a fig Newton but much more grown-up. Like fig Newtons, they age well and acquire a soft, dense texture after 1 or 2 days. ▸

◂ Preheat your oven to 375°F (190°C). Lightly grease a 9-by-13-by-1-inch quarter sheet pan, and line the bottom and sides with parchment paper.

◂ **Make the coconut-oat crumble crust** In the bowl of a stand mixer fitted with the paddle attachment, combine all the ingredients, and mix them on low speed until the mixture resembles rustic sand, about 4 minutes.

◂ Transfer half the crumble to the prepared pan, disperse it evenly over the bottom of the pan, and press it in. Reserve the other half at room temperature to use for the topping. Bake the crust for 20 minutes, just until it browns at the edges. Remove the crust from the oven.

◂ **Make the date filling** In a small pot, combine the coffee, dates, and salt, and cook over medium heat, stirring constantly with a heatproof spatula. Bring the mixture to a simmer, and allow it to thicken a little. Remove the pot from the heat, and cool it for 15 minutes, or until you can safely transfer the mixture to a blender. Blend until it's smooth.

◄ Pour the filling into the cooled crust, and crumble the reserved crumble evenly over the top. Reduce the oven temp to 350°F (176°C). Bake until the top is browned and the filling caramelizes at the edges of the pan, about 30 minutes. Remove the bars from the oven and allow them to cool in the pan. Once they're completely cooled, carefully remove them from the pan by lifting the parchment paper at the sides. Cut into twelve squares.

◄ These bars keep very well, stored in a sealed container at room temperature. To store them stacked, place parchment in between layers of bars.

Bundt and Loaf Cakes

A simple slice of cake cut from a loaf or Bundt is the pinnacle of understated dessert.

There's something so confident about serving that to guests, a slice of cake that can stand on its own—without the frills of thick frostings or extra layers. It's one of my favorite ways to end a meal, and when I write recipes for cakes like the ones that follow, I often think of the scenarios in which they will be served; it helps me to imagine the final form of the recipe, a way for me to visualize the character of the cake that takes it beyond JUST A LOAF.

In staying true to my desire to leave the act of creaming butter in the past, I reconnected with my love for oil-based loaf cakes for this chapter. These cakes come together quickly, without a stand mixer, and thanks to the oil in the recipes they stay moist for days—if they last that long. The old standby carrot cake gets a revamp with savory olive oil and warming spices, and the often side-eyed zucchini bread is reborn thanks to almonds, almond flour, and a handful of sweet and chewy dates.

Many of the cake recipes in this chapter are inspired by my good friend Cheryl Day. We discuss all things baking often, comparing recipes and talking about trends—me from my home in Los Angeles and her from Savannah, Georgia. Cheryl has written several baking books, and many of her recipes have that effortlessly classic feeling that I appreciate so much. Behind those recipes is a lot of intention. When she was working on *Cheryl Day's Treasury of Southern Baking,* she sent me an early copy, and I found a recipe that really excited me for a Cold Oven Pound Cake.

The method intrigued me: Place your cake in a totally cold oven, close the door, and then turn on the heat. As the oven preheats with the cake inside it, the batter tempers and slowly begins to cook. By the end of the bake time, the inside is a textbook-tight crumb, in my opinion one of the signs of a well-baked pound cake.

This may not be a time-saving hack, but it does a wonderful thing for the dense crumb of a pound or Bundt cake. The outside of the cake takes on an even golden color, and the outer inch of cake is still moist, not dry and overbaked—something that's often troubled me about the standard method of baking a pound cake.

Though the final cake in this chapter is neither a loaf nor a Bundt, it is one of the nicest simple cakes I can think of, and a perfect way to use extra-juicy fruits that perhaps have ripened past their prime snacking stage. Sunken Fruit Cake, or "buckle," is a rich batter of vanilla cake dimpled with berries macerated in honey. The juicy berries are intended to sink and leave a stain in the batter, the true sign of a good buckle. ■

Zucchini and Date Loaf Cake

MAKES ONE 9 × 5 INCH LOAF CAKE

6.5 ounces (180g) zucchini or other summer squash

⅓ cup (66g) granulated sugar, + more for coating the pan and topping the cake

1½ cups (187g) unbleached all-purpose flour

½ cup (50g) almond flour

1 teaspoon (4g) baking powder

½ teaspoon (3g) baking soda

1½ teaspoons (6g) ground cinnamon

¼ teaspoon (1g) ground nutmeg

1 teaspoon (3g) Diamond Crystal kosher salt

½ cup (112g) unrefined extra-virgin coconut oil

3 tablespoons (42g) unsalted butter

¼ cup packed (53g) dark-brown sugar

2 large eggs (100g)

2 teaspoons (10g) vanilla extract

1 cup (135g) chopped medjool dates

¼ cup (22g) sliced almonds

Z ucchini bread is often viewed as a consolation prize for growing too many summer squash, an easy way to sneak vegetables into cake and get them out of your fridge. To me, the subtle green sweetness of zucchini is welcome in a cake just as it is, but it's even better with dates, warm spices, and a crisp sliced-almond topping. ▶

◀ Grate the zucchini on the large holes of a box grater. Lay the grated zucchini in a single layer on several layers of paper towel or a folded kitchen cloth. Place a layer of paper towel or kitchen cloth over the top, and gently pat down to blot some of the moisture. Leave the zucchini like this while you prepare the rest of the batter.

◀ Preheat your oven to 350°F (176°C). Grease a 9-by-5-inch loaf pan, and coat the inside of the pan with granulated sugar.

◀ Whisk together the flour, almond flour, baking powder, baking soda, spices, and salt in a large mixing bowl; set it aside.

◀ Put the coconut oil and butter in a small saucepan, and warm the mixture over low heat until it's melted. Combine the melted oil and butter with the sugars, eggs, vanilla, and half of the chopped dates in a blender (or a large pitcher if you're using an immersion blender), and pulse until the dates are blended throughout.

◀ Make a well in the center of the flour mixture, and add the wet ingredients and the remaining chopped dates. Fold the wet into the dry, just until no bits of flour remain. Add the drained zucchini, and mix until everything is combined.

◀ Transfer the batter to the prepared loaf pan. Tap the loaf pan on the counter a few times to burst any air pockets. Sprinkle the top of the cake with granulated sugar and sliced almonds. Bake the cake until a toothpick or wooden skewer inserted in the center of the loaf comes out with a few moist crumbs clinging to it, about 1 hour. The cake will be tall and puffy, and browned at the edges, and the sliced almonds will be browned on top.

◀ Cool the cake in the pan for 30 minutes before removing it. Cool it completely before cutting. This cake keeps well wrapped in plastic or in a sealed container for up to 1 week.

MAKES ONE 9 × 5 INCH LOAF CAKE

7 ounces (200g) carrots

½ cup (100g) granulated sugar,
    + more for coating the pan
    and topping the cake

1¾ cups (218g) unbleached
    all-purpose flour

1 teaspoon (4g) baking powder

½ teaspoon (3g) baking soda

2 teaspoons (8g) ground cinnamon

¼ teaspoon (1g) ground nutmeg

1 teaspoon (2g) ground ginger

1 teaspoon (3g) Diamond
    Crystal kosher salt

½ cup (118ml) extra-virgin olive oil

½ cup packed (106g) dark-brown sugar

2 large eggs (100g)

2 teaspoons (10g) vanilla extract

1 cup (114g) chopped pecans, toasted

A simple carrot cake is one of the things that first put my name on the map. I was working at a restaurant in Venice, California, and I wanted to make an easy menu item that could be baked in advance and pulled out of the fridge when needed. Carrot cake happens to be the perfect cake to fill those needs: it gets better with age and tastes great cold. In loaf form, this cake is a wonderful breakfast treat; I like to spread a little sunflower-seed butter on my slice. ▶

◀ Grate the carrots on the large holes of a box grater; you will have about 1½ packed cups of grated carrot. Lay it in a single layer on several layers of paper towel or a folded kitchen cloth. Place a layer of paper towel or kitchen cloth over the top, and gently pat down to blot some of the moisture. Leave the carrot like this while you prepare the rest of the batter.

◀ Preheat your oven to 350°F (176°C). Grease a 9-by-5-inch loaf pan, and coat the inside of the pan with granulated sugar.

◀ Whisk together the flour, baking powder, baking soda, spices, and salt in a large mixing bowl; set it aside.

◀ Combine the oil with the sugars, eggs, and vanilla in a medium bowl, and whisk them into a smooth emulsion.

◀ Make a well in the center of the flour mixture, and add the wet ingredients. Fold the wet into the dry just until no bits of flour remain. Add the drained carrot and two-thirds of the chopped pecans and mix until everything is combined.

◀ Transfer the batter to the prepared loaf pan. Tap the loaf pan on the counter a few times to burst any air pockets. Sprinkle the top of the cake with granulated sugar and the remaining chopped pecans. Bake the cake until a toothpick or wooden skewer inserted in the center of the loaf comes out with a few moist crumbs clinging to it, 50 minutes to 1 hour. The cake will be tall and puffy and browned at the edges, the pecans will be deeply toasted, and the sugary top will be shiny and a little browned.

◀ Cool the cake in the pan for 30 minutes before removing it. Cool it completely before cutting. This cake keeps well wrapped in plastic or in a sealed container for up to 1 week.

Carrot and Olive Oil Loaf Cake

Lemony Greek Yogurt Pound Cake

MAKES ONE 9 × 5 INCH LOAF CAKE

4 ounces (113g) cold unsalted butter, cubed, + more for buttering the pan

1 cup (200g) granulated sugar, + more for coating the pan

4 tablespoons (24g) grated lemon zest

2 cups (250g) unbleached all-purpose flour

1 teaspoon (4g) baking powder

½ teaspoon (3g) baking soda

½ teaspoon (1.5g) Diamond Crystal kosher salt

2 large eggs (100g)

1½ cups (360g) plain full-fat Greek yogurt

Using Greek yogurt in pound cake creates a perfect sturdy but tender crumb. This cake narrowly walks the line between sweet and savory, and is a nice alternative to a super-rich and sweet traditional pound cake. One of my favorite ways to serve it is with olive-oil ice cream and roasted figs.

This cake is baked using the "Cold Oven" technique of placing your cake into a totally cold oven, closing the door, and then turning on the heat. It takes a little bit longer to bake, but produces a wonderfully even and golden color on the outside of the cake. ▶

◀ Generously butter a 9-by-5-inch loaf pan, and coat the inside of the pan with sugar. Combine the 1 cup sugar and the lemon zest in a small bowl, and rub the zest into the sugar with your fingers until the sugar is bright yellow and fragrant.

◀ In the bowl of a stand mixer fitted with the paddle attachment, mix the flour, baking powder, baking soda, lemon sugar, and salt together, to disperse the soda and powder and break up any lumps of sugar. Add the cold butter, and mix on low speed until the mixture resembles rustic sand, about 4 minutes.

◀ Whisk the eggs and Greek yogurt together in a small bowl, and slowly add this to the buttery mixture on low speed. Mix until everything is combined, making sure there are no dry bits of flour remaining.

◀ Transfer the batter to the prepared loaf pan. Tap the loaf pan on the counter a few times to burst any air pockets. Place the cake into a cold oven, on a center rack. Turn the oven on to 350°F (176°C). Bake the cake until a toothpick or wooden skewer inserted in the center of the loaf comes out with a few moist crumbs clinging to it, 50 minutes to 1 hour. The cake will be tall and puffy and browned at the edges.

◀ Cool the cake in the pan for 30 minutes before removing it. Cool it completely before cutting. This cake keeps well wrapped in plastic or in a sealed container for up to 1 week.

MAKES ONE 10 INCH (10–13-CUP) BUNDT CAKE

For the Cake

6 ounces (170g) cold unsalted butter, cubed, + more for buttering the pan

3 cups (375g) unbleached all-purpose flour, + more for coating the pan

½ cup (46g) unsweetened shredded coconut

1½ teaspoons (6g) baking powder

¾ teaspoon (4.5g) baking soda

1 teaspoon (3g) Diamond Crystal kosher salt

1¾ cups (350g) granulated sugar

3 tablespoons (42g) unrefined extra-virgin coconut oil

3 large eggs (150g)

1 cup (236ml) full-fat coconut milk, shaken

2 teaspoons (10g) vanilla bean paste

For the Glaze

¼ cup (59g) full-fat coconut milk, shaken

1 cup (115g) sifted confectioners' sugar

The irresistible aroma of coconut and butter is like a siren call to me. I love to serve a slice of this cake toasted, with some berries and whipped cream, for a simple dessert that looks unassuming but is guaranteed to blast your taste buds with a layered harmony of flavor.

This cake is baked using the "Cold Oven" technique of placing your cake in a totally cold oven, closing the door, and then turning on the heat. It takes a little bit longer to bake, but produces a wonderfully even and golden color on the outside of the cake. ▶

◀ Generously butter a 10-inch (10–13-cup) Bundt cake pan, and coat the inside of the pan with flour.

◀ **Make the cake** In the bowl of a stand mixer fitted with the paddle attachment, mix the flour, coconut, baking powder, baking soda, salt, and sugar together, to disperse the soda and powder and break up any lumps of sugar. Add the cold butter and coconut oil, and mix on low speed until the mixture resembles rustic sand, about 4 minutes.

◀ Whisk the eggs, coconut milk, and vanilla bean paste together in a small bowl, and slowly add this to the buttery mixture on low speed. Mix until everything is combined, making sure there are no dry bits of flour remaining.

◀ Transfer the batter to the prepared Bundt pan. Tap the pan on the counter a few times to burst any air pockets. Place the cake into a cold oven, on a center rack. Turn the oven on to 350°F (176°C). Bake the cake until a toothpick or wooden skewer inserted in the center comes out with a few moist crumbs clinging to it, about 1 hour and 15 minutes. The cake will be tall and puffy and browned at the edges.

◀ Cool the cake in the pan for 30 minutes before removing it. Let the cake continue cooling while you make the glaze.

◀ **Make the coconut glaze** In a small bowl, whisk 2 tablespoons of coconut milk into the confectioners' sugar to form a smooth, thick paste. Add the rest of the coconut milk, and whisk to combine it.

◀ Pour the glaze over the cooled cake. This cake keeps well at room temperature wrapped in plastic or in a sealed container for up to 1 week.

Vanilla and Coconut Bundt Cake

Crunchy Peanut Butter Bundt Cake

For the Cake

6 ounces (170g) cold unsalted butter, cubed, + more for buttering the pan

3 cups (375g) unbleached all-purpose flour, + more for coating the pan

1½ teaspoons (6g) baking powder

¾ teaspoon (4.5g) baking soda

1¾ cups (350g) granulated sugar

1 teaspoon (3g) Diamond Crystal kosher salt

3 large eggs (150g)

½ cup (135g) smooth peanut butter

1¼ cups (295ml) full-fat buttermilk

2 teaspoons (10g) vanilla extract

½ cup (64g) chopped peanuts, toasted, + more for decorating

For the Glaze

¼ cup (60g) whole milk

1 cup (115g) sifted confectioners' sugar

2 tablespoons (33g) smooth peanut butter

After years of being a pastry chef, I find that dessert at home has, unfortunately, become something of an afterthought. I find myself scrounging for a little something after dinner and often reaching for a spoon and a jar of crunchy peanut butter to kill the craving. This lightly salted, dense cake is my homage to my late-night scrounge. Want to ascend to PB heaven? Serve this warmed with chocolate ice cream and a handful of crushed salted peanuts.

This cake is baked using the "Cold Oven"' technique of placing your cake into a totally cold oven, closing the door, and then turning on the heat. It takes a little bit longer to bake, but produces a wonderfully even and golden color on the outside of the cake. ▶

◀ Generously butter a 10-inch (10–13-cup) Bundt cake pan, and coat the inside of the pan with flour.

◀ **Make the cake** In the bowl of a stand mixer fitted with the paddle attachment, mix the 3 cups flour, baking powder, baking soda, sugar, and salt together, to disperse the soda and powder and break up any lumps of sugar. Add the cold butter, and mix on low speed until the mixture resembles rustic sand, about 4 minutes.

◀ In a medium mixing bowl, whisk the eggs into the peanut butter until the combination is smooth; add the buttermilk and vanilla, and whisk to combine them. Slowly add the peanut-butter mixture to the dry ingredients, on low speed. Add the chopped peanuts, and mix until everything is combined.

◀ Transfer the batter to the prepared Bundt pan. Tap the loaf pan on the counter a few times to burst any air pockets. Place the cake into a cold oven, on a center rack. Turn the oven on to 350°F (176°C). Bake the cake until a toothpick or wooden skewer inserted in the center comes out with a few moist crumbs clinging to it, about 1 hour and 15 minutes. The cake will be tall and puffy and browned at the edges.

◀ Cool the cake in the pan for 30 minutes before removing it. Let the cake continue cooling while you make the glaze.

◀ **Make the peanut butter glaze** In a small bowl, whisk 2 tablespoons of milk into the confectioners' sugar to form a smooth, thick paste. Add the rest of the milk and the peanut butter, and whisk to combine it.

◀ Pour the glaze over the cooled cake. Top with a few small handfuls of chopped peanuts. This cake keeps well at room temperature wrapped in plastic or in a sealed container for up to 1 week.

For the Cake

6 ounces (170g) cold unsalted butter,
  cubed, + more for buttering the pan

3 cups (375g) unbleached all-purpose
  flour, + more for coating the pan

1 teaspoon (4g) baking powder

1 cup (200g) granulated sugar

1½ cups packed (320g) light-brown sugar

1 teaspoon (3g) Diamond
  Crystal kosher salt

4 large eggs (200g)

1 cup (236ml) full-fat milk

¼ cup (64g) full-fat sour cream

2 cups (380g) blueberries,
  + more for decorating

For the Glaze

¼ cup (59ml) whole milk

1 cup (115g) sifted confectioners' sugar

W hen I first made this brown-sugar-flavored Bundt cake, I got the same unsolicited reaction from all my friends: "It tastes like breakfast!" I decided to lean into that and toss in some blueberries.

This cake is baked using the "Cold Oven" technique of placing your cake into a totally cold oven, closing the door, and then turning on the heat. It takes a little bit longer to bake, but produces a wonderfully even and golden color on the outside of the cake. ►

◄ Generously butter a 10-inch (10–13-cup) Bundt cake pan, and coat the inside of the pan with flour.

◄ **Make the cake** In the bowl of a stand mixer fitted with the paddle attachment, mix the 3 cups flour, baking powder, sugars, and salt together, to disperse the powder and break up any lumps of sugar. Add the cold butter, and mix on low speed until the mixture resembles rustic sand, about 4 minutes.

◄ Whisk the eggs, milk, and sour cream together in a medium bowl, and slowly add this to the buttery mixture, beating on low speed. Remove the bowl from the stand mixer, and fold in half the blueberries.

◄ Transfer the batter to the prepared Bundt pan. Tap the pan on the counter a few times to burst any air pockets. Sprinkle the remaining blueberries over the surface of the cake batter. Place the cake into a cold oven, on a center rack. Turn the oven on to 350°F (176°C). Bake the cake until a toothpick or wooden skewer inserted in the center comes out with a few moist crumbs clinging to it, about 1 hour and 15 minutes. The cake will be tall and puffy and browned at the edges.

◄ Cool the cake in the pan for 30 minutes before removing it. Let the cake continue cooling while you make the glaze.

◄ **Make the blueberry glaze** In a small bowl, whisk 2 tablespoons of milk into the confectioners' sugar to form a smooth, thick paste. Add the rest of the milk and a couple of blueberries, using the whisk to crush the blueberries into the glaze, and whisk to combine it.

◄ Pour the glaze over the cooled cake. This cake keeps well at room temperature wrapped in plastic or in a sealed container for up to 1 week.

Blueberry and Brown Sugar Bundt Cake

Sour Cream Chocolate Chunk Bundt Cake

6 ounces (170g) cold unsalted butter,
cubed, + more for buttering the pan

3 cups (375g) unbleached all-purpose
flour, + more for coating the pan

1½ teaspoons (6g) baking powder

¾ teaspoon (4.5g) baking soda

1¾ cups (350g) granulated sugar

1 teaspoon (3g) Diamond
Crystal kosher salt

3 large eggs (150g)

1 cup (256g) full-fat sour cream

½ cup (118ml) full-fat buttermilk

1 cup (170g) roughly chopped
72% chocolate

1 tablespoon (7g) confectioners' sugar

A chocolate-chip cake was one of my favorites when I was a child, and, thanks to social media, I was reminded of this long-lost love when a fave baker I follow posted a sour-cream-based chocolate-chip Bundt cake. I sent the video cake to all the bakers at work, and we all agreed we needed to bake one someday soon. A few months later, on my birthday, I was presented with a perfect Sour Cream Chocolate Chunk Bundt Cake—much to my surprise, because I had once again forgotten about it! Never again: it is now part of my repertoire and should become part of yours, too.

This cake is baked using the "Cold Oven" technique of placing your cake into a totally cold oven, closing the door, and then turning on the heat. It takes a little bit longer to bake, but produces a wonderfully even and golden color on the outside of the cake. ▶

◀ Generously butter a 10-inch (10–13-cup) Bundt cake pan, and coat the inside of the pan with flour.

◀ In the bowl of a stand mixer fitted with the paddle attachment, mix the 3 cups flour, baking powder, baking soda, sugar, and salt together, to disperse the soda and powder and break up any lumps of sugar. Add the cold butter, and mix on low speed until the mixture resembles rustic sand, about 4 minutes.

◀ Whisk the eggs, sour cream, and buttermilk together in a medium bowl, and slowly add this to the butter and dry ingredients, with the mixer running on low speed. Remove the bowl from the stand mixer, and fold in half the chocolate.

◀ Transfer the batter to the prepared Bundt pan. Tap the pan on the counter a few times to burst any air pockets. Sprinkle the remaining chocolate over the surface of the cake batter. Place the cake into a cold oven, on a center rack. Turn the oven on to 350°F (176°C). Bake the cake until a toothpick or wooden skewer inserted in the center comes out with a few moist crumbs clinging to it, about 1 hour and 15 minutes. The cake will be tall and puffy and browned at the edges.

◀ Cool the cake in the pan for 30 minutes before removing it. Cool it completely before cutting. Before serving, place the confectioners' sugar in a sieve and dust the top of the cake. This cake keeps well wrapped in plastic or in a sealed container for up to 1 week.

MAKES ONE 10 INCH (10–13-CUP) BUNDT CAKE

For the Cinnamon-Pecan Streusel

4 ounces (113g) cold unsalted butter, cubed, + more for buttering the pan

½ cup (62g) unbleached all-purpose flour, + more for coating the pan

1¼ cups packed (266g) light-brown sugar

1 tablespoon (12g) ground cinnamon

1 teaspoon (3g) Diamond Crystal kosher salt

2 cups (228g) chopped pecans, toasted

For the Cake Batter

3 cups (375g) unbleached all-purpose flour

1½ teaspoons (6g) baking powder

¾ teaspoon (4.5g) baking soda

1¾ cups (350g) granulated sugar

1 teaspoon (3g) Diamond Crystal kosher salt

6 ounces (170g) cold unsalted butter, cubed

3 large eggs (150g)

1 cup (256g) full-fat sour cream

½ cup (118ml) full-fat buttermilk

For the Glaze

¼ cup (59ml) whole milk

1 cup (115g) sifted confectioners' sugar

There are few things better than a scrumptious, well-spiced coffee cake, but one of those things is a Sour Cream Pecan Coffee BUNDT Cake. I think the increased surface area of the Bundt pan really does a lot for the coffee cake genre, giving us more golden-brown cake flavor—and the hefty structure of a sturdy crumb makes for an indulgent treat.

This cake is baked using the "Cold Oven" technique of placing your cake into a totally cold oven, closing the door, and then turning on the heat. It takes a little bit longer to bake, but produces a wonderfully even and golden color on the outside of the cake. ▶

◀ Generously butter a 10-inch (10–13-cup) Bundt cake pan, and coat the inside of the pan with flour.

◀ **Make the cinnamon-pecan streusel** In the bowl of a stand mixer fitted with the paddle attachment, mix the cold butter, flour, brown sugar, cinnamon, and salt until you have a crumbly rubble with some small chunks of butter visible. Add the pecans, and toss the mixture to incorporate them. Transfer a quarter of the streusel to the prepared pan, creating a thin layer of streusel in the bottom. Transfer the remaining streusel to a medium bowl, and reserve it for later.

◀ **Make the cake batter** In the bowl of a stand mixer fitted with the paddle attachment, mix the flour, baking powder, baking soda, sugar, and salt together, to disperse the soda and powder and break up any lumps of sugar. Add the cold butter, and mix on low speed until the mixture resembles rustic sand, about 4 minutes.

◀ Whisk the eggs, sour cream, and buttermilk together in a medium bowl, and slowly add this to the butter and dry ingredients, with the mixer running on low speed.

◀ Transfer a third of the batter to the prepared Bundt pan. Tap the pan on the counter a few times to burst any air pockets. Sprinkle half the remaining streusel over the surface of the cake batter, and finish with the remaining cake batter. Reserve the rest of the streusel for later.

◀ Place the cake into a cold oven, on a center rack. Turn the oven on to 350°F (176°C). Bake the cake until a toothpick or wooden skewer inserted in the center comes out with a few moist crumbs clinging to it, about 1 hour and 15 minutes. The cake will be tall and puffy and browned at the edges.

◀ **Make the glaze** In a small bowl, whisk 2 tablespoons of milk into the confectioners' sugar to form a smooth, thick paste. Add the rest of the milk and whisk to combine it.

◀ Pour the glaze over the cooled cake, and top with the remaining streusel. This cake keeps well at room temperature wrapped in plastic or in a sealed container for up to 1 week.

Sour Cream Pecan Coffee Bundt Cake

Sunken
Fruit Cake

4 ounces (113g) cold unsalted butter, cubed, + more for buttering the pan

2 cups (380g) mixed berries, such as raspberries, blueberries, and boysenberries

2 tablespoons (42g) wildflower honey

4 cups (500g) unbleached all-purpose flour

½ teaspoon (2g) baking powder

½ teaspoon (3g) baking soda

1½ cups (300g) granulated sugar

½ cup packed (106g) light-brown sugar

1 teaspoon (3g) Diamond Crystal kosher salt

4 large eggs (200g)

1 cup (256g) full-fat sour cream

1 cup (236ml) full-fat buttermilk

1 teaspoon (5g) vanilla bean paste

1 tablespoon (7g) confectioners' sugar

A buckle was one of my signature cakes when I worked as pastry chef for the Gjelina Group. Every bite is tangy, tart, and deliciously rich. I love this cake with mixed berries, but using one single variety can also be nice. If you're serving it after dinner, add some fresh berries and a little whipped cream on the side. ▶

◀ Preheat your oven to 350°F (176°C). Generously butter a 12-by-9-inch casserole dish.

◀ Toss the berries in the honey in a medium bowl, and allow them to macerate while you mix the cake batter.

◀ In the bowl of a stand mixer fitted with the paddle attachment, mix the flour, baking powder, baking soda, sugars, and salt together, to disperse the soda and powder and break up any lumps of sugar. Add the cold butter, and mix on low speed until the mixture resembles rustic sand, about 4 minutes.

◀ Whisk the eggs, sour cream, buttermilk, and vanilla bean paste together in a medium bowl, and slowly add it to the butter and dry ingredients, with the mixer running on low speed. Mix until you have a smooth batter, about 2 minutes.

◀ Transfer half of the batter to the prepared casserole dish. Tap the dish on the counter a few times to burst any air pockets. Sprinkle half the macerating berries and any juices they've created over the surface of the cake batter. Top with the remaining batter, followed by the rest of the berries and juices. Bake the cake on the center rack of your oven until it's browned and set in the center and the berry juices bubble a little at the sides, about 1 hour.

◀ Cool the cake in the pan for 1 hour. Before serving, place the confectioners' sugar in a sieve and dust the top of the cake.

◀ This cake is great with ice cream or crème fraîche. Store leftovers in a sealed container in the fridge for up to 1 week.

04

Five Distinct Banana Bread Recipes

The ubiquitous banana-bread loaf: Is it health food? Is it just cake, wearing a mask of wholesomeness?

The origins of this iconic "bread" are actually far more practical. In the late 1920s, bananas were becoming more easily available, and by the time the Depression hit, every home cook was looking for ways to make use of every scrap of food. At the same time, baking powder became widely available, presenting home cooks with a slew of quick and easy recipes. Banana bread was one of these recipes, and has gone through many evolutions since.

I think banana bread deserves more respect. It is a workhorse in the baking canon, but if you love it as much as I do, you know that not all banana breads are created equal. Sometimes, in an effort to skew into health-food territory, this loaf cake can easily become gummy and gluey textured. That's not the banana bread for me. I prefer to admire banana bread for what it is, a cake that's acceptable to eat for breakfast. I want a loaf that's sweet, but not too sweet, and tastes like banana—which, oddly enough, is not always the case with banana bread.

I have tried to cover all the bases of banana-bread styles in this mini-chapter, but, as with the chocolate-chip cookie, it's hard to limit yourself. I begin with the banana-bread recipe of my youth, so I call it Classic 1980s Mom Banana Bread, a simple, nourishing loaf that is a perfect snacking cake. From that base, I developed a slightly more grown-up version with Browned Butter Banana Bread, which includes hazelnuts and a little espresso. Then, desiring something slightly more virtuous than just cake, I worked on a Wholesome Hi-Protein Banana Bread, because we can all use more protein in our diets—but we still need cake.

"What about chocolate and banana?" you might find yourself asking right about now. Of course, I needed a bit of chocolate, a classic pairing, so a Chocolate Marbled Banana Bread was necessary. To close out this mini-chapter, I have included my favorite banana-bread recipe of recent years, Spicy Streusel-Covered Banana Bread, a coffee-cake-adjacent loaf that, once you start snacking on, you might not be able to stop. ■

Classic 1980s Mom Banana Bread

4 medium (472g) very ripe bananas

⅔ cup (158ml) neutral oil,
    such as grapeseed, + more
    for greasing the pan

1 cup packed (213g) dark-brown sugar

1 teaspoon (5g) vanilla extract

2 large eggs (100g)

⅓ cup (85g) full-fat sour cream

1½ cups (187g) unbleached
    all-purpose flour

1 teaspoon (6g) baking soda

1 teaspoon (4g) baking powder

1 teaspoon (4g) ground cinnamon

¼ teaspoon (1g) ground nutmeg

1 teaspoon (3g) Diamond
    Crystal kosher salt

1 cup (114g) roughly chopped walnuts
    or pecans, toasted (optional)

3 tablespoons (36g) demerara sugar

had to start the banana-bread chapter with the version closest to my heart, a banana bread that keeps it classic, utilizing what I think of as the hallmarks of a good banana-bread recipe: melted or liquid fat, sour cream or yogurt, and a crunchy baked sugar-top crust. The pecans are an optional addition; I would have picked them out of a slice as a child, but I've come to love them as an adult. ▶

◀ Preheat your oven to 350°F (176°C). Lightly oil a 9-by-5-inch loaf pan, and line it with parchment paper.

◀ In a large mixing bowl, smash the bananas, using the back of a fork or a potato masher. Add the oil, brown sugar, vanilla, eggs, and sour cream. Whisk to combine everything.

◀ Whisk together the flour, baking soda, baking powder, cinnamon, nutmeg, and salt in a small bowl. Fold this into the banana mixture until it's just combined. Add the nuts, if using, and mix to combine them; then transfer the batter to your prepared pan. Sprinkle the surface with the demerara sugar.

◀ Bake it for 40 to 50 minutes, on the center rack of your oven, until a skewer inserted in the center comes out clean and the top of the cake has set and is browned. Leave it to cool in the pan for about 30 minutes, then transfer it to a wire rack to cool completely. Store leftovers at room temperature in a sealed container for up to 1 week.

¼ cup (59ml) neutral oil, such as
grapeseed, + more for oiling the pan

3 ounces (85g) unsalted butter

4 medium (472g) very ripe bananas

1 cup packed (213g) dark-brown sugar

1 teaspoon (5g) vanilla extract

2 large eggs (100g)

1 tablespoon (9g) instant
espresso powder mixed with
2 tablespoons hot water

⅓ cup (85g) full-fat sour cream

1½ cups (187g) unbleached
all-purpose flour

1 teaspoon (6g) baking soda

1 teaspoon (4g) baking powder

1 teaspoon (3g) Diamond
Crystal kosher salt

½ cup (71g) blanched hazelnuts, toasted
and lightly crushed (optional)

3 tablespoons (36g) demerara sugar

There is nothing wrong with the classic banana-bread recipe (page 100), but sometimes I want a more complex version, and that's when I introduce the flavor superpowers of espresso, browned butter, and toasted hazelnuts. This strong loaf needs a strong topping, and for that I look to extra-crunchy demerara sugar. ▶

◀ Preheat your oven to 350°F (176°C). Lightly oil a 9-by-5-inch loaf pan, and line it with parchment paper.

◀ Melt the butter in a small saucepan set over medium heat, and continue cooking, while scraping the bottom of the pot with a heatproof spatula, until the butter is browned and nutty-smelling. Transfer the browned butter and all the browned bits to a heatproof bowl to cool for 15 minutes before using it.

◀ In a large mixing bowl, smash the bananas with the back of a fork or a potato masher. Add the browned butter, oil, brown sugar, vanilla, eggs, espresso, and sour cream. Whisk to combine everything.

◀ Whisk together the flour, baking soda, baking powder, and salt in a small bowl. Fold this into the banana mixture until it's just combined. Add three-quarters of the hazelnuts, if using, and mix to combine them; then transfer the batter to your prepared pan. Sprinkle the surface with the demerara sugar and the remaining hazelnuts.

◀ Bake it for 40 to 50 minutes, on the center rack of your oven, until a skewer inserted in the center comes out clean and the top of the cake has set and is browned. Leave it to cool in the pan for about 30 minutes, then transfer it to a wire rack to cool completely. Store leftovers at room temperature in a sealed container for up to 1 week.

Browned Butter Banana Bread

Wholesome Hi-Protein Banana Bread

MAKES ONE 9 × 5 INCH LOAF

½ cup (113g) unrefined extra-virgin coconut oil, warmed so that it is liquid, + more for oiling the pan

4 medium (472g) very ripe bananas, + 1 large banana (118g) for topping the loaf

⅓ cup (64g) coconut sugar

⅓ cup (40g) vanilla-flavored protein powder

2 large eggs (100g)

½ cup (120g) plain low-fat Greek yogurt

⅔ cup (83g) unbleached all-purpose flour

¾ cup (72g) almond flour

½ teaspoon (3g) baking soda

2 teaspoons (8g) baking powder

2 teaspoons (8g) ground cinnamon

1 teaspoon (3g) Diamond Crystal kosher salt

3 tablespoons (36g) demerara sugar (optional)

Banana bread may not be a health food, but it can be nourishing. Though not low in calories, this loaf is giving about 24g protein per slice, a nice bonus for something that tastes so good. I originally came up with this version of banana bread with my husband, Blaine, in mind, who loves to do long-distance bike rides and never eats enough before, during, or after them. With lots of natural sweetness from banana and coconut sugar, this makes a great snack that gives you a little boost mid-ride or mid-hike. ▶

◀ Preheat your oven to 350°F (176°C). Lightly oil a 9-by-5-inch loaf pan, and line it with parchment paper.

◀ In a large mixing bowl, smash 4 medium bananas, using the back of a fork or a potato masher. Add the oil, coconut sugar, protein powder, eggs, and Greek yogurt. Whisk to combine everything.

◀ Whisk together the flour, almond flour, baking soda, baking powder, cinnamon, and salt in a small bowl. Fold this into the banana mixture until everything is just combined; then transfer the batter to your prepared pan. Cut the additional banana as desired (in half, into slices, whatever you want) and place it on the surface of the batter. Sprinkle the top with the demerara sugar, if using.

◀ Bake it for 40 to 50 minutes, on the center rack of your oven, until a skewer inserted in the center comes out clean and the top of the cake has set and is browned. Leave it to cool in the pan for about 30 minutes, then transfer it to a wire rack to cool completely. Store leftovers at room temperature in a sealed container for up to 1 week.

MAKES ONE 9 x 5 INCH LOAF

⅔ cup (156ml) neutral oil, such as grapeseed, + more for oiling the pan

4 medium (472g) very ripe bananas

1 cup packed (213g) dark-brown sugar

1 teaspoon (5g) vanilla extract

2 large eggs (100g)

⅓ cup (85g) full-fat sour cream

1½ cups (187g) unbleached all-purpose flour

1 teaspoon (6g) baking soda

1 teaspoon (4g) baking powder

1 teaspoon (4g) ground cinnamon

¼ teaspoon (1g) ground nutmeg

1 teaspoon (3g) Diamond Crystal kosher salt

½ cup (85g) dark-chocolate chunks

¼ cup (21g) cocoa powder, Dutch-processed or natural

3 tablespoons (37g) granulated sugar

A marble pound cake met a loaf of banana bread, and YET ANOTHER VARIATION on our muse (banana bread) was created. A rich and chocolatey swirling of banana bread and the essence of "box mix" chocolate cake sets this confidently in dessert territory. A toasted slice with some lightly sweetened whipped cream draped over the top makes for a low-effort—high-payoff after-dinner treat. ▶

◀ Preheat your oven to 350°F (176°C). Lightly oil a 9-by-5-inch loaf pan, and line it with parchment paper.

◀ In a large mixing bowl, smash the bananas, using the back of a fork or a potato masher. Add the oil, brown sugar, vanilla, eggs, and sour cream. Whisk to combine everything.

◀ Whisk together the flour, baking soda, baking powder, cinnamon, nutmeg, and salt in a small bowl. Fold this into the banana mixture until it's just combined. Add the chocolate chunks, and mix to combine them.

◀ Pour half the batter into a clean bowl, and add the cocoa powder; stir with a spoon until the cocoa powder is just combined. Scoop out about ¼ cup of the plain batter, and dollop it into a corner of the prepared pan. Do the same with the chocolate batter, placing the dollop next to the plain batter. Repeat this pattern, alternating dollops of plain batter, then chocolate batter, into the loaf pan, covering the bottom of the pan and then layering them on top of each other, until there's no batter remaining.

◀ Use a butter knife or wooden dowel to create a marbled swirl—running the knife side to side in a figure eight down the length of the pan while gently lifting the knife up in a swirly motion. One pass of swirls is enough—too much swirling will cause the batters to get mixed together, and you will lose the distinct marbled effect. Sprinkle the surface with the granulated sugar.

◀ Bake it for 1 hour, on the center rack of your oven, until a skewer inserted in the center comes out clean and the top of the cake has set and has browned. Leave it to cool in the pan for about 30 minutes, then transfer it to a wire rack to cool completely. Store leftovers at room temperature in a sealed container for up to 1 week.

Chocolate Marbled Banana Bread

Spicy Streusel-Covered Banana Bread

For the Batter

3 ounces (85g) unsalted butter,
+ more for buttering the pan

4 medium (472g) very ripe bananas

¼ cup (59ml) neutral oil,
such as grapeseed

1 cup packed (213g) dark-brown sugar

1 teaspoon (5g) vanilla extract

2 large eggs (100g)

⅓ cup (85g) full-fat sour cream

1½ cups (187g) unbleached
all-purpose flour

1 teaspoon (6g) baking soda

1 teaspoon (4g) baking powder

1 tablespoon (9g) ground ginger

2 teaspoons (8g) ground cinnamon

1 teaspoon (3g) Diamond
Crystal kosher salt

For the Streusel

¼ cup (31g) unbleached all-purpose flour

3 tablespoons packed (40g)
dark-brown sugar

1 teaspoon (3g) ground ginger

1 teaspoon (4g) ground cinnamon

Pinch of Diamond Crystal kosher salt

2 tablespoons (25g) neutral
oil, such as grapeseed

To wrap up what might be the only banana bread *chapter* ever allowed to be published in a cookbook, I present my favorite version. Spicy, textural, and just rich enough for me, this banana bread tastes almost tropical, thanks to the ginger in both the cake and the streusel—a reminder that the magical *Musa acuminata* is actually a tropical fruit. ▶

◀ Preheat your oven to 350°F (176°C). Butter a 9-by-5-inch loaf pan, and line it with parchment paper.

◀ **Make the batter** Melt the butter in a small saucepan set over medium heat, and continue cooking, while scraping the bottom of the pot with a heatproof spatula, until it's browned and nutty-smelling. Transfer the browned butter and all the browned bits to a heatproof bowl to cool for 15 minutes before using it.

◀ In a large mixing bowl, smash the bananas with the back of a fork or a potato masher. Add the browned butter, oil, brown sugar, vanilla, eggs, and sour cream. Whisk to combine everything.

◀ Whisk together the flour, baking soda, baking powder, ginger, cinnamon, and salt in a small bowl. Fold this into the banana mixture until it's just combined, then pour the batter into your prepared pan.

◀ **Make the streusel** Whisk together the flour, brown sugar, spices, and salt in a small bowl. Add the oil and mix until you have a sandy crumble.

◀ Scatter the crumble over the top of the batter. Bake it for 40 to 50 minutes, on the center rack of your oven, until a skewer inserted in the center comes out clean and the top of the cake has set and is browned. Leave it to cool in the pan for about 30 minutes, then transfer it to a wire rack to cool completely. Store leftovers at room temperature in a sealed container for up to 1 week.

Fruit Pies, Handpies, Galettes

To me, peak pie season starts in spring and goes until Thanksgiving.

The real sweet spot, though, is during the blurry rush of summer—when the softer fruits hit the farmers' market tables, and berries are displayed next to peaches and some early apples. I am not usually much of a collector, but summer fruit really gets my FOMO going, and I start buying everything I can get my hands on, even if I don't have a particular use for it. Three flats of black raspberries? I will take them. A special on dappled plums? I'll freeze some to use later, an insurance policy for the drab winter months. Most of the fruit we buy at the bakery during this time gets immediately turned into pies.

There have been some remarkable combinations as a result of my wild fruit-buying strategy, some of them seeing the bakery case for only one week, when the ingredients overlap. Rhubarb with Raspberry, Vanilla, and Blood Orange Pie (page 136) is a favorite that comes to mind. The sweet and sensual white peach doesn't make an interesting pie on its own because of its lack of acid; it would be best served raw and eaten out of hand. But with a handful of black raspberries, it becomes a vehicle for a really special flavor. Black raspberries taste just OK eaten raw, but when they're combined with some sugar and some heat, a complex, floral, and candylike flavor is coaxed out.

With great fruit, the possibilities for building on flavor feel endless. This is something I love to play with at home, where I can create bespoke flavor poetry more freely than at the bakery, thanks to a well-stocked garden and the freedom to bake to my own personal taste instead of wondering if my customers will appreciate my esoteric combinations. If you are as tired of classic apple pie as I am, maybe I can inspire you to season your next one with toasted fig leaves and vanilla bean (page 122), a combination that to me tastes like a snapshot of a season shifting from late summer to early fall.

The pie section must begin with pie dough, because without the crust there would be no pie. "There would be a cobbler or a crisp!" you could reason, and, yes, that could be true. But it wouldn't be a pie.

I started making pies relatively late in my pastry career, and that is probably why I have very little loyalty to pie-related lore. I did not learn to bake a pie from either of my grandmothers. Instead, pies are something that I taught myself. First, I learned what I loved about pie by eating a lot of it, and then I moved on to the source of most of my knowledge surrounding baking: cookbooks.

For many years, I have tinkered with various methods of making pie dough, and of teaching others to make it. Time and time again, the methodology I preached left even the most experienced bakers feeling unsupported in their pie-making journey. There are a lot of warnings when it comes to making a great crust: don't let the dough get too hot, don't touch it too much, don't forget to rest it for two hours, but even better if overnight . . . Are you feeling anxious yet? I am.

I used to make pie dough by hand, using the fraisage method of incorporating the butter into the flour. This is a wonderful way to make pastry, until it gets hot in the summer or you are a woman over forty who all of a sudden has hot hands. When the fraisage method goes well, it creates beautiful long sheets of butter trapped in just-strong-enough gluten, replicating a layering system very close to puff pastry and a very flaky dough. When it goes wrong, the butter melts and coats too much of the flour, preventing the liquid from penetrating the dough, and you end up with underhydrated dough that cracks when you roll it and is texturally short and pasty when it's baked.

Now, though, the Cold Butter Method (page 4) is the key to my pie dough. Using a stand mixer allows me to incorporate the cold fat effortlessly into the flour and break that fat down to exactly the right point before adding the liquid. Something that is harder to do when working by hand.

I once posted a video of me online making a forty-pound batch of dough by hand. Lots of people thought I was cool. One guy commented, "Why not just use a machine?"—which pissed me right off, because at the time I really thought I needed to do this work by hand. Now here I am, years later, happily mixing pie dough in my stand mixer. ■

MAKES 2 PORTIONS OF DOUGH, ENOUGH FOR 2 SINGLE-CRUST PIES OR 1 DOUBLE-CRUST PIE

2 tablespoons packed (26g) dark-brown sugar

2 teaspoons (10g) apple-cider vinegar

1 teaspoon (3g) Diamond Crystal kosher salt

2 ounces (60ml) cold water

2¾ cups (343g) unbleached all-purpose flour, + more for rolling

8 ounces (226g) cold unsalted butter, cubed

This recipe is the basis of both my bakery and my reputation as a baker. It has traveled with me from job to job and, finally, to my own business, Fat + Flour. I used this crust recipe when I won four out of seven blue ribbons at the KCRW Good Food Piefest & Contest, a moment that shaped my career, and again when I won a blue ribbon in the National Pie Contest, which cemented my future in pie.

The method has changed over time, but the ratio of the measurements has always stayed the same. The secret to this recipe is two points in the process: dissolving the sugar and salt in the water, so that every speck of flour is hydrated by seasoned liquid; and using a stand mixer for a mostly hands-off mixing with just enough power to develop the right amount of gluten while keeping the dough cool. ▶

◀ In a measuring cup, combine the brown sugar, vinegar, salt, and water. Use a spoon to stir the mixture until the sugar and salt have dissolved. Chill the liquid in the freezer until it's very cold but not frozen, and keep it in the fridge until you're ready to use it.

◀ In a stand mixer fitted with the paddle attachment, mix the flour and cold butter on low speed until the mixture resembles uneven pebbles with a few larger pieces of butter throughout, about 2 to 4 minutes.

◀ Slowly add the cold liquid to the bowl, with the mixer running on low speed. Continue mixing on low speed until a chunky, shaggy dough forms and no dry bits remain, about 30 seconds.

◀ Lightly dust a counter or cutting board with flour. Turn the dough out onto the counter, and gently knead it a few times, to bring it together into a cohesive dough. Shape the dough into a rectangle about 6 by 8 inches.

◀ Lightly dust a rolling pin with flour. Position the dough with the short side facing you. While it is still pliable but cool, roll the dough out to an 8-by-12-inch rectangle.

◀ Fold the bottom third of the dough two-thirds of the way toward the top.

◀ Fold the remaining third of the dough down, so that it is on top of the rest of the dough, like you would fold a letter.

◀ Cut the dough down the center into two portions, each of them measuring about 4 by 4 inches.

◀ Wrap each portion of dough well in plastic, and gently round the corners to form each into a somewhat circular shape. Chill the dough for a minimum of 1 hour. Once it has chilled, you can roll it out and use it in any pastry-crust pie or handpie recipe. Unbaked dough can be kept frozen for up to 3 months.

Fat + Flour
Pie Dough

Vegan Fat + Flour Pie Dough

MAKES **2** PORTIONS OF DOUGH,
ENOUGH FOR 2 SINGLE-CRUST PIES OR
1 DOUBLE-CRUST PIE

2 tablespoons packed (26g)
    dark-brown sugar

2 teaspoons (10g) apple-cider vinegar

1 teaspoon (3g) Diamond
    Crystal kosher salt

2 ounces (60ml) cold water

2¾ cups (343g) unbleached all-
    purpose flour, + more for rolling

8 ounces (226g) frozen unsalted
    vegan butter, such as Violife
    Plant Butter, cubed

I jumped at the chance to convert my pie dough recipe to one without dairy butter. I had tried before, using vegetable shortening, but gave up when, no matter how I worked with it, the dough came out pale and crumbly—a result of the lack of water in vegan shortening. Advances in vegan butters have made it a lot easier, because they behave more and more like dairy butter in baking recipes these days. Even so, vegan fats still require working with in a slightly different way. Every ingredient in this recipe needs to be frozen or ice cold, and using the mixer really helps control the temperature of the dough so that the vegan butter doesn't break down too fast while you're mixing. When you nail the mixing of this dough, it's almost impossible to tell that it's vegan. ▶

◀ In a measuring cup, combine the brown sugar, vinegar, salt, and water. Use a spoon to stir the mixture until the sugar and salt have dissolved. Chill the liquid in the freezer until it's very cold but not frozen, and keep it in the fridge until you're ready to use it. Transfer the flour to a bowl, and freeze it for 30 minutes.

◀ In a stand mixer fitted with the paddle attachment, mix the flour and butter on low speed until the mixture resembles uneven pebbles with a few larger pieces of butter throughout, about 2 to 4 minutes. Put the mixture in the freezer and chill it for 10 minutes, to make sure it is still very cold, before proceeding with the recipe.

◀ Return the bowl to the stand mixer. With the mixer running on low speed, add the cold liquid to the bowl. Continue mixing until a chunky, shaggy dough forms and no dry bits remain, about 30 seconds of mixing on low speed.

◄ Lightly dust a counter or cutting board with flour. Turn the dough out onto the counter, and gently knead it a few times to bring it together into a cohesive dough. Shape the dough into a rectangle about 6 by 8 inches.

◄ Lightly dust a rolling pin with flour. Position the dough with the short side facing you. While it is still pliable but cool, roll the dough out to an 8-by-12-inch rectangle.

◄ Fold the bottom third of the dough two-thirds of the way toward the top.

◄ Fold the remaining third of the dough down, so that it is on top of the rest of the dough, like you would fold a letter.

◄ Cut the dough down the center, into two portions, each of them measuring 4 by 4 inches.

◄ Wrap each portion of dough well with plastic, and gently round the corners to form each into a somewhat circular shape. Chill the dough for a minimum of 1 hour. Once it has chilled, you can roll it out and use it in any pastry-crust pie or handpie recipe. Unbaked dough can be kept frozen for up to 3 months.

Crimping a "Perfect" Crust

Every pie crust is a signature of the baker. I find that this part of the pie baking process is where most newbies become scared or nervous that their pie crust won't be "perfect," and it's always the part of the process that people want to watch me do over and over again. Like most good things, practice makes progress, and if you set your mind on crimping "perfect" crusts, you will surely find what YOUR perfect looks like, and master it. Here is how I crimp my crust or sign my signature, if you will:

Once my pie dough has rested and been rolled to a 12-inch round, I place it in my pie tin. I use my fingers to ease the dough into the bend at the base of the tin, the warmth from my hands relaxing the cold pie dough into place.

Once the dough is settled, and I have an even border of pie dough hanging over the circumference of the tin, I use my pointer finger and thumb on my left hand to roll the border of dough toward the inside of the pie tin while I use my pointer finger and thumb on my right hand to pinch the rolled dough.

I continue around the rim of the tin, rolling inward and pinching, until I have reached the start and I have a border that resembles a rope.

Once I have my rope border, I start my crimp. I place the knuckle of my left pointer finger and the tip of my thumb on the inside edge of the roped border.

I use the tip of my thumb on my right hand to press down into the pie tin edge and into the space between my left knuckle and thumb, like a cog on a gear system fitting into place.

I move my fingers over one space, placing the tip of my left thumb into the space where my left knuckle previously was, and repeat the process until I have crimped around the entire circumference of the pie tin.

You could stop here, your crust is crimped and ready to proceed with the recipe. I like to go around the crimped border once more, opening the crimped sections a little with my thumb and pointer finger while pressing them into the edge of the tin. ∎

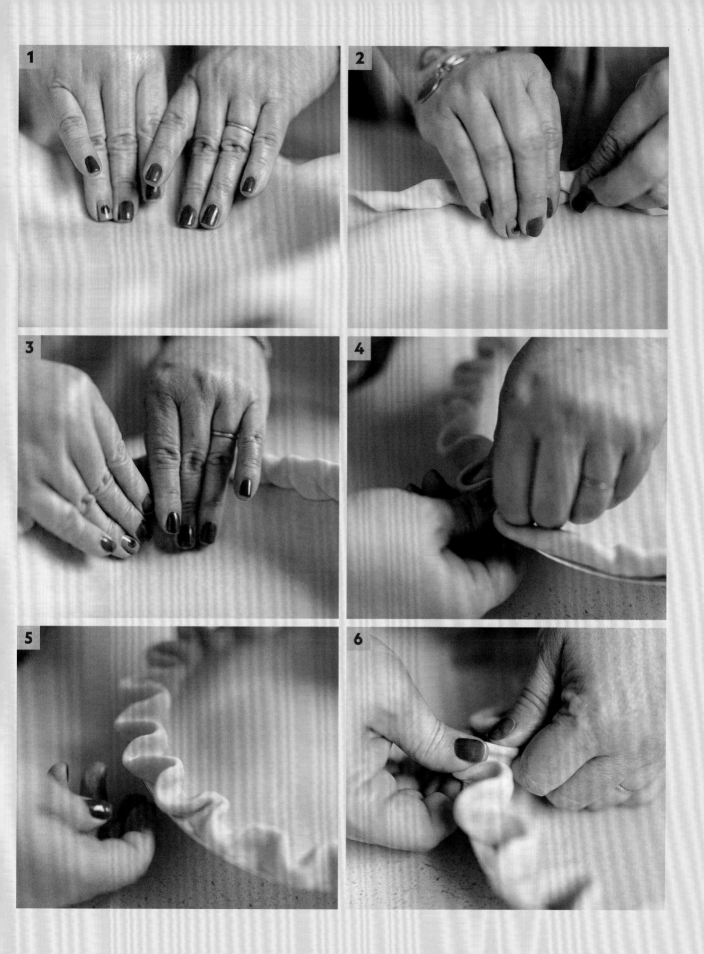

Summer Apple Pie with Fig Leaf and Vanilla

For the Filling

2½ pounds (1.36kg) tart summer apples, such as Mutsu, Gravenstein, or Pink Lady

1 cup (200g) granulated sugar, + more for decorating

1 teaspoon (3g) Diamond Crystal kosher salt

2 tablespoons (20g) cornstarch

1 tablespoon (15g) pear brandy (optional)

1 tablespoon (15g) ground toasted fig leaf (see Note, page 71)

2 teaspoons (10g) vanilla bean paste

To Assemble the Pie

Unbleached all-purpose flour for rolling the dough

1 recipe Fat + Flour Pie Dough (page 114) or Vegan Fat + Flour Pie Dough (page 118), made in advance and chilled

1 teaspoon (5g) toasted ground fig leaf (see Note, page 71)

3 tablespoons (42g) heavy cream

I dreamed up this pie during the fledgling tail end of summer, when apples arrive at the market and figs are ripening but not quite ready. It's still summer, so to me it's not quite the right time for the typical rich, warmly spiced, brown-sugar-flavored classic apple pie. This version is tart and clean-tasting, filled with bright apples, the round, green, coconutty aroma of fig leaves in the sun, and luxurious vanilla bean. ▶

◀ **Make the filling** Peel and core the apples, and slice them ¼ inch thick. Combine the apples with the sugar, salt, cornstarch, brandy (if using), fig leaf, and vanilla bean paste in a large mixing bowl. Toss the apples gently so that they are well coated in this mixture. Cover the bowl with a kitchen towel or plastic wrap and let it sit at room temperature for 20 minutes.

◀ Preheat your oven to 375°F (190°C). Line a baking sheet with parchment paper.

◀ **Assemble the pie** Lightly flour a work surface. Remove the dough from the fridge, and remove the plastic. If your dough has been chilled overnight, it will need to temper before being rolled; this usually takes 10 to 15 minutes. Once the dough is pliable, roll one disc out to a 12-inch circle. Use flour throughout the rolling process as needed to prevent sticking. Transfer the rolled dough to a 9-inch pie plate, and trim the edge to allow 1 inch of dough to hang over the edge. Roll or fold the hanging edge of the dough over itself, using your thumb and forefinger to crimp the edge. Put the crimped crust into the freezer while you roll the top crust.

◀ Lightly flour your work surface again, and roll the second disc of dough out to a 10-inch circle.

◀ Remove the crimped crust from the freezer, and pour the filling in. Pour all the juices that may have collected in the bottom of the bowl over the apples. Place the top crust gently over the apples, and use your thumb to press the top crust into the bottom crust. Cut a few slashes in the top of the pie.

◀ Whisk the ground fig leaf and sugar together in a small bowl. Brush the top crust of the pie generously with the heavy cream, and sprinkle it with the fig-leaf sugar. Chill the whole pie in the freezer for 10 minutes, transfer it to the prepared baking sheet, then place the pie into your preheated oven, on the center rack, and bake it until the crust is a deep golden brown and the juices from the pie are boiling. This should take 1 full hour, and possibly longer. Cool the pie for 2 hours before eating, to allow the juices to settle and continue thickening. Store any leftovers in the fridge, and warm slices of the cold pie at 375°F (190°C) for 15 minutes before eating, for best results.

Buttery Apple Pie with Fall Spices

MAKES ONE **9** INCH PIE

For the Filling

2½ pounds (1.36kg) apples (choose a
blend of seasonal varieties, such as
Pink Lady, Fuji, Empire, or Jonathan)

1 cup packed (213g) dark-brown sugar

1½ teaspoons (4.5g) Diamond
Crystal kosher salt

2 tablespoons (20g) cornstarch

2 teaspoons (8g) ground cinnamon

¼ teaspoon (1g) ground nutmeg

1 teaspoon (3g) ground ginger

4 ounces (113g) unsalted butter, melted

To Assemble the Pie

Unbleached all-purpose flour
for rolling the dough

1 recipe Fat + Flour Pie Dough (page 114),
made in advance and chilled

3 tablespoons (42g) heavy cream

3 tablespoons (38g) granulated sugar

Unlike the Summer Apple Pie with Fig Leaf and Vanilla (page 122), this one is classic—and perfect as the closer for a hearty cold-weather meal. Full of sweet and juicy apples, dark-brown sugar, and lots of warming spices and butter—it has that textbook American Apple Pie flavor and aroma. ▶

◀ **Make the filling** Peel and core the apples, slice them ¼ inch thick, and transfer them to a large mixing bowl. Whisk the brown sugar, salt, cornstarch, and spices together in a small bowl. Add the melted butter, and whisk to combine everything. Pour this over the sliced apples, and toss so that they are well coated. Cover the bowl with a kitchen towel or plastic wrap, and let it sit at room temperature for 20 minutes.

◀ Preheat your oven to 375°F (190°C). Line a baking sheet with parchment paper.

◀ **Assemble the pie** Lightly flour a work surface. Remove the dough from the fridge, and remove the plastic. If your dough has been chilled overnight, it will need to temper before being rolled; this usually takes 10 to 15 minutes. Once the dough is pliable, roll one disc out to a 12-inch circle. Use flour throughout the rolling process as needed to prevent sticking. Transfer the rolled dough to a 9-inch pie plate, and trim the edge to allow 1 inch of dough to hang over the edge. Roll or fold the hanging edge of the dough over itself, using your thumb and forefinger to crimp the edge. Put the crimped crust into the freezer while you roll the top crust.

◀ Lightly flour your work surface again, and roll the second disc of dough out to a 10-inch circle.

◀ Remove the crimped crust from the freezer, and pour the filling in. Pour all the juices that may have collected in the bottom of the bowl over the apples. Place the top crust gently over the apples, and use your thumb to press the top crust into the crimped crust. Cut a few slashes in the top of the pie.

◀ Brush the top crust of the pie generously with the heavy cream, and sprinkle it with the sugar. Chill the whole pie in the freezer for 10 minutes, transfer it to the prepared baking sheet, then place the pie into your preheated oven, on the center rack, and bake it until the crust is a deep golden brown and the juices from the pie are boiling. This should take 1 full hour, and possibly longer. Cool the pie for 2 hours before eating, to allow the juices to settle and continue thickening. Store any leftovers in the fridge, and warm slices of the cold pie at 375°F (190°C) for 15 minutes before eating, for best results.

For the Filling

2 pounds (906g) tart summer apples, such as Mutsu, Gravenstein, or Pink Lady

1 cup (200g) granulated sugar, + more for decorating

6 leaves of fresh lemon verbena

1 teaspoon (3g) Diamond Crystal kosher salt

3 tablespoons (30g) cornstarch

1 cup (123g) black raspberries (or red raspberries if black not available)

To Assemble the Pie

Unbleached all-purpose flour for rolling the dough

1 recipe Fat + Flour Pie Dough (page 114), made in advance and chilled

3 tablespoons (42g) cold unsalted butter

3 tablespoons (42g) heavy cream

E arthy black raspberries, tart summer apples, and floral lemon verbena are a powerhouse combo that is unique and also familiar. We get so few black raspberries on the West Coast that when they hit the market I usually buy several flats and freeze them, with the intention of making this pie. Lemon verbena can be found dried in most spice shops as an herbal tea, and fresh plants of verbena are available at many garden shops; it's very easy to grow and makes a great tea. ▶

◀ **Make the filling** Peel and core the apples, and slice them ¼ inch thick. Place the sugar and lemon verbena into a large mixing bowl, and rub the leaves into the sugar. Do this until all the leaves have been softened by the rubbing and the sugar is very fragrant. Whisk the verbena sugar, salt, and cornstarch together in a large bowl. Add the sliced apples, and toss together so that they are well coated. Let the fruit macerate while you prepare the crust.

◀ Preheat your oven to 375°F (190°C). Line a baking sheet with parchment paper.

◀ **Assemble the pie** Lightly flour a work surface. Remove the dough from the fridge, and remove the plastic. If your dough has been chilled overnight, it will need to temper before being rolled; this usually takes 10–15 minutes. Once the dough is pliable, roll one disc out to a 12-inch circle. Use flour throughout the rolling process as needed to prevent sticking. Transfer the rolled dough to a 9-inch pie plate, and trim the edge to allow 1 inch of dough to hang over the edge. Roll or fold the hanging edge of the dough over itself, using your thumb and forefinger to crimp the edge. Put the crimped crust into the freezer while you roll the top crust.

◀ Lightly flour your work surface again, and roll the second disc of dough out to a 10-inch circle.

◀ Add the black raspberries to the apples, and gently stir them in, trying not to break them up too much. Remove the crimped crust from the freezer, and pour the filling in. Pour all the juices that may have collected in the bottom of the bowl over the filling. Break up the butter with your fingers, and dot the surface of the filling with it. Place the top crust gently over the fruit, and use your thumb to press the top crust into the crimped crust. Cut a few slashes in the top of the pie.

◀ Brush the top crust of the pie generously with the heavy cream, and sprinkle it with the sugar. Chill the whole pie in the freezer for 10 minutes, transfer it to the prepared baking sheet, then place the pie into your preheated oven, on the center rack, and bake it until the crust is a deep golden brown and the juices from the pie are boiling. This should take 1 full hour, and possibly longer. Cool the pie for 2 hours before eating, to allow the juices to settle and continue thickening. Store any leftovers in the fridge, and warm slices of the cold pie at 375°F (190°C) for 15 minutes before eating, for best results.

Tart Apple with Black Raspberry and Lemon Verbena Pie

Sesame Crumble Apple Pie

For the Filling

2½ pounds (1.36kg) apples (choose a blend of seasonal varieties, such as Pink Lady, Fuji, Empire, or Jonathan)

¾ cup packed (160g) dark-brown sugar

1½ teaspoons (4.5g) Diamond Crystal kosher salt

2 tablespoons (20g) cornstarch

1 tablespoon (10g) white sesame seeds, toasted

3 tablespoons (63g) tahini

3 tablespoons (42g) cold water

¼ cup (84g) wildflower honey

2 tablespoons (28g) lemon juice

For the Sesame Crumble

1 cup (125g) unbleached all-purpose flour

¼ cup packed (53g) light-brown sugar

¼ cup (50g) granulated sugar

½ teaspoon (1.5g) Diamond Crystal kosher salt

1 tablespoon (10g) white sesame seeds, toasted

½ cup (113g) unsalted butter, melted and cooled

When I had my restaurant, Fiona, I made this apple-sesame pie for the one and only Thanksgiving we were open. To me, the combo of sesame and bright apples is similar to browned butter and apples—a match made in fruit heaven. Unfortunately, several customers were upset by the lack of "normal apple" pie on my menu and wrote me angry emails about it. Wouldn't be the last time that happened—certainly was not the first, either. What matters is that the Sesame Crumble Apple Pie remains, and if you are a fan of both these flavors, you will be delightfully surprised by their flavor when combined. ▶

◀ **Make the filling** Peel and core the apples, and slice them ¼ inch thick. Whisk the brown sugar, salt, cornstarch, and sesame seeds together in a large bowl. Add the apples, and toss. Whisk the tahini, water, honey, and lemon juice together in a small bowl, and add this to the apples. Gently toss the mixture so all the apple slices are coated.

◀ **Make the sesame crumble** Whisk the flour, sugars, salt, and sesame seeds together in a medium bowl, add the melted butter, and mix until a buttery crumble forms. Set it aside.

◀ Preheat your oven to 375°F (190°C). Line a baking sheet with parchment paper.

◀ **Assemble the pie** Lightly flour a work surface. Remove the dough from the fridge, and remove the plastic. If your dough has been chilled overnight, it will need to temper before being rolled; this usually takes 10 to 15 minutes. Once the dough is pliable, roll the disc out to a 12-inch circle. Use flour throughout the rolling process as needed to prevent sticking. Transfer the rolled dough to a 9-inch pie plate, and trim the

Unbleached all-purpose flour for rolling the dough

½ recipe Fat + Flour Pie Dough (page 114), made in advance and chilled

edge to allow 1 inch of dough to hang over the edge. Roll or fold the hanging edge of the dough over itself, using your thumb and forefinger to crimp the edge. Put the crimped crust into the freezer for 20 minutes.

◄ Pour the filling and all the juices that may have collected in the bottom of the bowl into the crust. Scatter the sesame crumble over the top of the apples.

◄ Chill the whole pie in the freezer for 10 minutes, transfer it to the prepared baking sheet, then place the pie into your preheated oven, on the center rack, and bake it until the crust is a deep golden brown and the juices from the pie are boiling. This should take 1 full hour, and possibly longer. Cool the pie for 2 hours before eating, to allow the juices to settle and continue thickening. Store any leftovers in the fridge, and warm slices of the cold pie at 375°F (190°C) for 15 minutes before eating, for best results.

Mulled Wine, Quince, and Apple Pie

For the Filling

2 cups (473ml) mulled wine,
  store-bought or homemade

1 pound (453g) quince

1 pound (453g) apples (choose a blend
  of seasonal varieties, such as Pink
  Lady, Fuji, Empire, or Jonathan)

1 cup (200g) granulated sugar

1 teaspoon (3g) Diamond
  Crystal kosher salt

3 tablespoons (30g) cornstarch

To Assemble the Pie

Unbleached all-purpose flour
  for rolling the dough

1 recipe Fat + Flour Pie Dough (page 114),
  made in advance and chilled

3 tablespoons (42g) cold unsalted butter

3 tablespoons (42g) heavy cream

3 tablespoons (38g) granulated sugar

love the heady floral aroma of quince mingling with apple and spices, and this recipe is a perfect, super-classy alternative to a traditional apple pie. Poaching the quince in mulled wine gives them an even rosier red color, and the resulting pie is complex in flavor. ▶

◀ **Make the filling** Put the mulled wine into a medium saucepan. Peel and core the quince, and slice them ¼ inch thick; add them to the mulled wine, and bring it to a simmer. Cook the quince until the slices are fork-tender, about 30 minutes. Remove the quince slices, and cool them to room temperature. Continue simmering the mulled wine until it has reduced to a thin syrup that has the viscosity of maple syrup, about 15 minutes. Cool the mulled wine syrup to room temperature before continuing with the recipe.

◀ Peel and core the apples, and slice them ¼ inch thick. Whisk the sugar, salt, and cornstarch together in a large mixing bowl. Add the sliced apples, cooked quince, and ¼ cup mulled wine syrup and gently toss it so that all the fruit is well coated.

◀ Preheat your oven to 375°F (190°C). Line a baking sheet with parchment paper.

◀ **Assemble the pie** Lightly flour a work surface. Remove the dough from the fridge, and remove the plastic. If your dough has been chilled overnight, it will need to temper before being rolled; this usually takes 10 to 15 minutes. Once the dough is pliable, roll one disc out to a 12-inch circle. Use flour throughout the rolling process as needed to prevent sticking. Transfer the rolled dough to a 9-inch pie plate, and trim the edge to allow 1 inch of dough to hang over the edge. Roll or fold the hanging edge of the dough over itself, using your thumb and forefinger to crimp the edge. Put the crimped crust into the freezer while you roll the top crust.

◀ Lightly flour your work surface again, and roll the second disc of dough out to a 10-inch circle. Remove the crust from the freezer. Pour the filling and all the juices that may have collected in the bottom of the bowl into the crust. Break up the butter with your fingers, and dot the surface of the fruit with it. Place the top crust gently over the fruit, and use your thumb to press the top crust into the crimped crust. Cut a few slashes in the top of the pie.

◀ Brush the top crust of the pie generously with the heavy cream, and sprinkle it with the sugar. Chill the whole pie in the freezer for 10 minutes, transfer it to the prepared baking sheet, then place the pie into your preheated oven, on the center rack, and bake it until the crust is a deep golden brown and the juices from the pie are boiling. This should take 1 full hour, and possibly longer. Cool the pie for 2 hours before eating, to allow the juices to settle and continue thickening. Store any leftovers in the fridge, and warm slices of the cold pie at 375°F (190°C) for 15 minutes before eating, for best results.

Unbleached all-purpose flour
for rolling the dough

½ recipe Fat + Flour Pie
Dough (page 114), made in
advance and chilled

1½ pounds (680g) apples (choose
a blend of seasonal varieties,
such as Pink Lady, Mutsu,
Empire, or Jonathan)

½ cup (100g) granulated sugar,
+ more for decorating

1 tablespoon (15g) vanilla bean paste

1 tablespoon (10g) cornstarch

Pinch of Diamond Crystal kosher salt

2 tablespoons (28g) heavy cream

2 tablespoons (30g) apple jelly
or apricot preserves

Some dessert occasions call for something a little bit less rustic than a big comforting deep-dish pie. That's where the galette comes in, and apples are the perfect galette fruit, thanks to how they retain their shape after baking. The slices of apple in this recipe get tossed with vanilla bean and sugar, then glazed with reduced juices and a bit of jelly, for a finished look worthy of any fancy French pastry shop. ▶

◀ Preheat your oven to 375°F (190°C). Line a baking sheet with parchment paper.

◀ Lightly flour a work surface. Remove the dough from the fridge, and remove the plastic. If your dough has been chilled overnight, it will need to temper before being rolled; this usually takes 10 to 15 minutes. Once the dough is pliable, roll the disc out to a 12-inch circle. Use flour throughout the rolling process as needed to prevent sticking. Transfer the rolled dough to your prepared baking sheet.

◀ Use the tips of your fingers to roll the outer 1 inch of the crust into a rope shape, moving around the perimeter of the dough. See pictures (page 121) for more detail. Chill the prepared crust in the fridge while you prepare the apples.

◀ Peel and core the apples, and slice them ¼ inch thick. Whisk the sugar, vanilla bean paste, cornstarch, and salt together in a large bowl. Add the apples, and toss. Let the apples sit at room temperature for 15 minutes, so that some of the juices are drawn out.

◀ **To assemble the galette** Starting in the center of the chilled crust, place the apple slices in a spiral going all the way to the rolled edge. If you still have fruit left over once you have spiraled apples over the pastry, wedge the rest in between and around the edge. Use all the fruit! Once the fruit is placed, drizzle 3 tablespoons of the leftover juices from the bowl on top; reserve the rest of the juices for later.

◀ Brush the edges of the pastry with the heavy cream, and sprinkle it with the sugar. Bake it for about 30 minutes, on the center rack of your oven, until the crust is deeply golden brown. Rotate the baking sheet, and continue baking until the juices bubble in the center of the galette and the apples begin to caramelize, about 30 minutes. Mix the apple jelly with the reserved juices in a small saucepan. Bring the mixture to a simmer, and cook it over medium heat until it has thickened to a syrupy glaze; cool it to room temperature. Remove the galette from the oven, and allow it to cool on the baking sheet for 30 minutes, before brushing on the cooked glaze.

◀ Brush the top of the fruit with the jelly glaze to get a luscious, shiny surface. Serve it warm. Store any leftovers in the fridge, and warm slices of the cold galette at 375°F (190°C) for 7 minutes before eating, for best results.

Apple and Vanilla Galette

Gingery Pear Crumble Pie

MAKES ONE 9 INCH PIE

For the Ginger Crumble

1 cup (125g) unbleached all-purpose flour

¼ cup packed (53g) light-brown sugar

¼ cup (50g) granulated sugar

Pinch of Diamond Crystal kosher salt

2 tablespoons (30g) finely
   chopped candied ginger

½ cup (113g) unsalted butter,
   melted and cooled

To Assemble the Pie

Unbleached all-purpose flour
   for rolling the dough

½ recipe Fat + Flour Pie
   Dough (page 114), made in
   advance and chilled

For the Filling

2½ pounds (1.36kg) firm but
   fragrant pears, such as Bartlett,
   Green Anjou, or Comice

½ cup (100g) granulated sugar

1 teaspoon (3g) Diamond
   Crystal kosher salt

3 tablespoons (30g) cornstarch

3 tablespoons (63g) wildflower honey

2 tablespoons (28g) lemon juice

1 tablespoon (14g) bourbon (optional)

1 tablespoon (7g) freshly grated ginger

F un fact: There is a video on the internet somewhere of me teaching a celeb how to make a pear pie on late-night television; it includes an NSFW story about pears. If the internet still exists when you read this, search Nicole Rucker + Seth Meyers + Pears and see what comes up.

I love pears so much, but I find they really turn to mush if used when too ripe. So—the key to success is choosing pears that are ripe-ish but fragrant. This will ensure that you won't end up with (delicious) soggy baby food in a crumble and crust. It's very important not to allow the fruit to macerate in the sugar for any length of time, or else a lot of juices will be pulled out and you will have a li'l soupy situation. ▶

◀ **Make the crumble topping** Whisk the flour, sugars, salt, and candied ginger together in a small bowl; add the melted butter, and mix until it resembles a buttery crumble.

◀ Preheat your oven to 375°F (190°C). Line a baking sheet with parchment paper.

◀ **Assemble the pie** Lightly flour a work surface. Remove the dough from the fridge, and remove the plastic. If your dough has been chilled overnight, it will need to temper before being rolled; this usually takes 10 to 15 minutes. Once the dough is pliable, roll the disc out to a 12-inch circle. Use flour throughout the rolling process as needed to prevent sticking. Transfer the rolled dough to a 9-inch pie plate, and trim the edge to allow 1 inch of dough to hang over the edge. Roll or fold the hanging edge of the dough over itself, using your thumb and forefinger to crimp the edge. Put the crimped crust into the freezer while you prepare the filling.

◂ **Make the filling** Peel and core the pears, and slice them ¼ inch thick. Whisk the sugar, salt, and cornstarch together in a large bowl. Add the pears, and toss. Whisk the honey, lemon juice, bourbon (if using), and ginger together in a small bowl, and add this to the pears. Gently toss the mixture so all the fruit is coated.

◂ Immediately pour the filling and any juices that may have collected in the bottom of the bowl into the crust, and scatter the crumble over the top.

◂ Chill the whole pie in the freezer for 10 minutes, transfer it to the prepared baking sheet, then place the pie into your preheated oven, on the center rack, and bake it until the crust is a deep golden brown and the juices from the pie are boiling. This should take 1 full hour, and possibly longer. Cool the pie for 1 hour before eating, to allow the juices to settle and continue thickening. Store any leftovers in the fridge, and warm slices of the cold pie at 375°F (190°C) for 15 minutes before eating, for best results.

Rhubarb with Raspberry, Vanilla, and Blood Orange Pie

For the Filling

1½ pounds (680g) red rhubarb,
   cut into 1-inch chunks

1 cup (200g) granulated sugar

1 cup (120g) raspberries,
   hulled and sliced

1 tablespoon (6g) grated
   blood-orange zest

3 tablespoons (46g) blood-orange juice

2 teaspoons (10g) vanilla bean paste

1 teaspoon (3g) Diamond
   Crystal kosher salt

3 tablespoons (30g) cornstarch

To Assemble the Pie

1 recipe Fat + Flour Pie Dough (page 114),
   made in advance and chilled

Unbleached all-purpose flour
   for rolling the dough

3 tablespoons (42g) cold unsalted butter

3 tablespoons (42g) heavy cream

3 tablespoons (37g) granulated sugar

E very time I mix up this pie, I get a flashback to eating pink Starburst during lunchtime at school. Memories of the way the first few chomps make the back of your jaw twinge from the tartness, and the smell of the vanilla and fake berry flavoring come straight back to me. I love rhubarb on its own, and I still make a rhubarb pie several times a season for the real rhubarb lovers, but I can't deny that this combination has some power. I also enjoy making this pie in January without the raspberries; to do that, simply substitute an equal amount of rhubarb for the berries, and add 2 extra tablespoons of sugar. ▶

◀ **Make the filling** Combine the rhubarb and sugar in a large mixing bowl, cover the bowl with a tea towel or plastic wrap, and let it sit at room temperature for ½ hour.

◀ Preheat your oven to 375°F (190°C). Line a baking sheet with parchment paper.

◀ **Assemble the pie** Lightly flour a work surface. Remove the dough from the fridge, and remove the plastic. If your dough has been chilled overnight, it will need to temper before being rolled; this usually takes 10 to 15 minutes. Once the dough is pliable, roll one disc out to a 12-inch circle. Use flour throughout the rolling process as needed to prevent sticking. Transfer the rolled dough to a 9-inch pie plate, and trim the edge to allow 1 inch of dough to hang over the edge. Roll or fold the hanging edge of the dough over itself, using your thumb and forefinger to crimp the edge. Put the crimped crust into the freezer while you roll the top crust.

◀ Lightly flour your work surface again, and roll the second disc of dough out to a 10-inch circle.

◀ Add the sliced raspberries, orange zest, orange juice, vanilla bean paste, salt, and cornstarch to the rhubarb, and toss so that the fruit is well coated.

◀ Remove the crimped crust from the freezer, and pour the filling in, adding all the juices that may have collected in the bottom of the bowl over the filling. Break up the butter with your fingers, and dot the surface of the fruit with it. Place the top crust gently over the fruit, and use your thumb to press the top crust into the crimped crust. Cut a few slashes in the top of the pie.

◀ Brush the top crust of the pie generously with the heavy cream, and sprinkle it with the sugar. Chill the whole pie in the freezer for 10 minutes, transfer it to the prepared baking sheet, then place the pie into your preheated oven, on the center rack, and bake it until the crust is a deep golden brown and the juices from the pie are boiling. This should take 1 full hour, and possibly longer. Cool the pie for 2 hours before eating, to allow the juices to settle and continue thickening. Store any leftovers in the fridge, and warm slices of the cold pie at 375°F (190°C) for 15 minutes before eating, for best results.

For the Filling

¾ cup (150g) granulated sugar

2 teaspoons (2g) dried culinary lavender

1 teaspoon (3g) Diamond
   Crystal kosher salt

3 tablespoons (30g) cornstarch

1¾ pounds (794g) fresh blueberries

1 tablespoon (14g) lemon juice

For the Cream Cheese Crumble

1½ cups (187g) unbleached
   all-purpose flour

¼ cup packed (53g) light-brown sugar

¼ cup (50g) granulated sugar

½ teaspoon (1.5g) Diamond
   Crystal kosher salt

½ cup (113g) unsalted butter,
   melted and cooled

4 tablespoons (57g) cold
   plain cream cheese

To Assemble the Pie

Unbleached all-purpose flour
   for rolling the dough

½ recipe Fat + Flour Pie
   Dough (page 114), made in
   advance and chilled

4 tablespoons (57g) plain cream
   cheese, at room temperature

first made this pie while visiting my friends in Savannah, Georgia. I was in a very well stocked kitchen that included numerous botanical ingredients for me to experiment with. I went for the tub of lavender sugar and a bottle of lavender hydrosol I found in the fridge. If you're worried about the floral element in this recipe overpowering, never fear, the lavender adds a little special note behind the blueberries that boosts them up. The cream cheese lining the crust and in the crumble makes for a tangy and tender variation, and helps to protect the bottom crust from the super-juicy berries. ▶

◀ **Make the filling** Add the sugar and lavender to a large mixing bowl, and use your fingers to rub the buds into the sugar and break them up. Add the salt, cornstarch, and half of the blueberries, and toss so all the fruit is coated. Place the remaining blueberries into the freezer. Let the coated fruit macerate for ½ hour. Transfer it and all its juices to a medium saucepan, and cook over medium heat until the juices boil and thicken. Remove the cooked filling from the heat, and transfer it to a heatproof bowl. Add the frozen blueberries and lemon juice, and stir.

◀ **Make the crumble topping** Whisk the flour, sugars, and salt together in a medium mixing bowl. Add the melted butter and cream cheese, and mix with a fork until it resembles a buttery crumble. Some small chunks of cream cheese are OK.

◀ Preheat your oven to 375°F (190°C). Line a baking sheet with parchment paper.

◀ **Assemble the pie** Lightly flour a work surface. Remove the dough from the fridge, and remove the plastic. If your dough has been chilled overnight, it will need to temper before being rolled; this usually takes 10–15 minutes. Once the dough is pliable, roll the disc out to a 12-inch circle. Use flour throughout the rolling process as needed to prevent sticking. Transfer the rolled dough to a 9-inch pie plate, and trim the edge to allow 1 inch of dough to hang over the edge. Roll or fold the hanging edge of the dough over itself, using your thumb and forefinger to crimp the edge. Put the crimped crust into the freezer for 20 minutes.

◀ Once the crust has chilled, smear the cream cheese onto the bottom of the pie crust, pour the filling over it, and add all the juices that may have collected in the bottom of the bowl. Scatter the crumble over the top.

◀ Chill the whole pie in the freezer for 10 minutes, transfer it to the prepared baking sheet, then place the pie into your preheated oven, on the center rack, and bake until the crust is a deep golden brown and the juices from the pie are boiling. This should take 1 full hour, and possibly longer. Cool the pie for 1 hour before eating, to allow the juices to settle and continue thickening. Store any leftovers in the fridge, and warm slices of the cold pie at 375°F (190°C) for 15 minutes before eating, for best results.

Blueberry with Lavender and Cream Cheese Crumble Pie

Blackberry and Buttery Oat Crumble Pie

For the Filling

¾ cup (150g) granulated sugar

1 teaspoon (3g) Diamond
   Crystal kosher salt

3 tablespoons (30g) cornstarch

1 teaspoon (4g) ground cinnamon

1¾ pounds (794g) fresh blackberries
   (or substitute boysenberries,
   marionberries, or a mixture
   of brambleberries)

1 tablespoon (15g) apple-cider vinegar

For the Crumble Topping

1 cup (125g) unbleached all-purpose flour

½ cup (45g) rolled oats

¼ cup packed (53g) light-brown sugar

¼ cup (50g) granulated sugar

Pinch of Diamond Crystal kosher salt

½ cup (113g) unsalted butter,
   melted and cooled

To Assemble the Pie

Unbleached all-purpose flour
   for rolling the dough

½ recipe Fat + Flour Pie
   Dough (page 114), made in
   advance and chilled

There is something so indulgent to me about a blackberry pie. It could be my childhood: blackberries were scarce in my life until I went to college and was able to buy my own food, and, naturally, I veered toward all the fancy fruits my family hadn't been able to afford when I was growing up. These days, I look to a blackberry pie when I desire a rich and jammy dessert, because blackberries mingle with butter in a way no other fruit does. There's an old trick in this recipe—adding a splash of vinegar to the pie to help break down the seeds. There is no way around them, though; if you want blackberry pie, you must accept the seeds. ▶

◀ **Make the filling** Whisk the sugar, salt, cornstarch, and cinnamon together in a large bowl. Add half of the berries, and toss so all the fruit is coated. Place the remaining berries into the freezer. Let the coated fruit macerate for ½ hour. Transfer the macerated fruit and all the juices to a medium saucepan, and cook over medium heat until the juices boil and thicken. Remove the cooked filling from the heat, and transfer it to a heatproof bowl. Add the frozen berries and the vinegar, and stir them in.

◀ **Make the crumble topping** Whisk the flour, oats, sugars, and salt together in a medium mixing bowl. Add the melted butter, and mix with a fork until it resembles a buttery crumble.

◀ Preheat your oven to 375°F (190°C). Line a baking sheet with parchment paper.

◀ **Assemble the pie** Lightly flour a work surface. Remove the dough from the fridge, and remove the plastic. If your dough has been chilled overnight, it will need to temper before being rolled; this usually takes 10 to 15 minutes. Once the dough is pliable, roll the disc out to a 12-inch circle. Use flour throughout the rolling process as needed to prevent sticking. Transfer the rolled dough to a 9-inch pie plate, and trim the edge to allow 1 inch of dough to hang over the edge. Roll or fold the hanging edge of the dough over itself, using your thumb and forefinger to crimp the edge. Put the crimped crust into the freezer for 20 minutes.

◀ Once the crust has chilled, pour the filling in, adding all the juices that may have collected in the bottom of the bowl. Scatter the crumble over the top.

◀ Chill the whole pie in the freezer for 10 minutes, transfer it to the prepared baking sheet, then place the pie into your preheated oven, on the center rack, and bake it until the crust is a deep golden brown and the juices from the pie are boiling. This should take 1 full hour, and possibly longer. Cool the pie for 1 hour before eating, to allow the juices to settle and continue thickening. Store any leftovers in the fridge, and warm slices of the cold pie at 375°F (190°C) for 15 minutes before eating, for best results.

Boysenberry and Lemon Galette

Unbleached all-purpose flour
   for rolling the dough

½ recipe Fat + Flour Pie
   Dough (page 114), made in
   advance and chilled

½ cup (100g) granulated sugar,
   + more for decorating

1 tablespoon (10g) cornstarch

Pinch of Diamond Crystal kosher salt

1 pound (453g) boysenberries

1 Meyer lemon, seeds removed, sliced
   very thinly with skin on (8–10 slices)

2 tablespoons (30g) heavy cream

2 tablespoons (60g) marmalade
   or apple jelly

I f I plan my summer well, I can stash away some boysenberries in the freezer so that I can make this galette when Meyer lemons start to arrive at the market. Berries and lemon make a common flavor profile, but I find that the bitter/sweet/textural combo of boysenberries and cooked lemon slices, specifically, provide a new experience that fruit lovers may not expect. This recipe is best made with Meyer lemons, because they have a nice thin skin that bakes well. A thicker-skinned lemon, like Eureka, will not break down enough and will be too chewy. ▶

◀ Preheat your oven to 375°F (190°C). Line a baking sheet with parchment paper.

◀ Lightly flour a work surface. Remove the dough from the fridge, and remove the plastic. If your dough has been chilled overnight, it will need to temper before being rolled; this usually takes 10 to 15 minutes. Once the dough is pliable, roll the disc out to a 12-inch circle. Use flour throughout the rolling process as needed to prevent sticking. Transfer the rolled dough to your prepared baking sheet. Use the tips of your fingers to roll the outer 1 inch of the crust into a rope shape, moving around the perimeter of the dough. See pictures (page 121) for more detail. Put the prepared crust in the fridge while you prepare the fruit.

◀ Whisk the sugar, cornstarch, and salt together in a large bowl. Add the berries and lemon slices, and toss.

◀ **To assemble the galette** Arrange the berries and lemon slices on the chilled crust, leaving a 2-inch perimeter free of fruit around the edges. If you still have fruit once you have covered the center of the pastry, try to add the rest of the fruit in the center and around the edge. Use all the fruit! Once the fruit is placed, drizzle any leftover juices from the bowl on top. Fold the exposed edge of the crust over the edge of the fruit in little pleats, working your way around the galette until all the crust has been folded over.

◀ Brush the edges of the pastry with the heavy cream, and sprinkle it with sugar. Bake on the center rack of the oven for about 30 minutes, until the crust is deeply golden brown, then rotate the baking sheet and continue baking until the juices bubble in the center of the galette and the lemon slices begin to caramelize, about 1 hour total. Remove the galette from the oven, and allow it to cool on the baking sheet.

◀ Meanwhile, mix the marmalade or jelly with 1 teaspoon hot water. After the galette has cooled for 30 minutes, brush the top of the fruit with the glaze to get a luscious, shiny surface. Serve it warm. Store any leftovers in the fridge, and warm slices of the cold pie at 375°F (190°C) for 15 minutes before eating, for best results.

Old-Fashioned Sour Cherry Pie with Bourbon

For the Filling

1 cup (200g) granulated sugar

1 teaspoon (3g) Diamond Crystal kosher salt

¼ cup (40g) cornstarch

2 teaspoons (8g) ground cinnamon

2½ pounds (1.36kg) pitted sour cherries, fresh or thawed frozen

3 tablespoons (42g) bourbon

2 teaspoons (10g) vanilla bean paste

2 teaspoons (4g) grated lemon zest

To Assemble the Pie

Unbleached all-purpose flour for rolling the dough

1 recipe Fat + Flour Pie Dough (page 114), made in advance and chilled

3 tablespoons (42g) heavy cream

3 tablespoons (37g) granulated sugar

'Ve always loved the *idea* of a cocktail with a cherry and some orange peel in it, but I never learned to love alcohol much. So I save my booze for pies like this, where the bourbon adds a really special burst of character to the sour cherry. During the season, you can often find someone in my bakery kitchen just DUMPING bourbon into a vat of cherry filling that smells like citrus peels and vanilla and sweet fruitiness. ▶

◀ **Make the filling** Whisk the granulated sugar, salt, cornstarch, and cinnamon together in a large mixing bowl. Add the cherries, bourbon, vanilla bean paste, and lemon zest, and toss so that the cherries are well coated. Set the filling aside.

◀ Preheat your oven to 375°F (190°C). Line a baking sheet with parchment paper.

◀ **Assemble the pie** Lightly flour a work surface. Remove the dough from the fridge, and remove the plastic. If your dough has been chilled overnight, it will need to temper before being rolled; this usually takes 10 to 15 minutes. Once the dough is pliable, roll one disc out to a 12-inch circle. Use flour throughout the rolling process as needed to prevent sticking. Transfer the rolled dough to a 9-inch pie plate, and trim the edge to allow 1 inch of dough to hang over the edge. Roll or fold the hanging edge of the dough over itself, using your thumb and forefinger to crimp the edge. Put the crimped crust into the freezer while you roll the top crust.

◄ Lightly flour your work surface again, and roll the second disc of dough out to a 10-inch circle.

◄ Remove the crimped crust from the freezer, and pour the filling in, adding all the juices that may have collected in the bottom of the bowl over the fruit. Place the top crust gently over the fruit, and use your thumb to press it into the crimped crust. Cut a few slashes in the top of the pie.

◄ Brush the top crust of the pie generously with the heavy cream, and sprinkle it with the sugar. Chill the whole pie in the freezer for 10 minutes, transfer it to the prepared baking sheet, then place the pie into your preheated oven, on the center rack, and bake it until the crust is a deep golden brown and the juices from the pie are boiling. This should take 1 full hour, and possibly longer. Cool the pie for 2 hours before eating, to allow the juices to settle and continue thickening. Store any leftovers in the fridge, and warm slices of the cold pie at 375°F (190°C) for 15 minutes before eating, for best results.

For the Filling

1½ pounds (680g) stone fruits
(apricots, plums, and peaches)

½ pound (226g) pitted cherries,
fresh or thawed frozen

3 tablespoons (42g) bourbon

2 teaspoons (10g) vanilla bean paste

2 teaspoons (4g) lemon zest

¾ cup (150g) granulated sugar

1 teaspoon (3g) Diamond
Crystal kosher salt

¼ cup (28g) cornstarch

2 teaspoons (8g) ground cinnamon

For the Crumble Topping

1 cup (125g) unbleached all-purpose flour

½ cup (45g) rolled oats

¼ cup packed (53g) light-brown sugar

¼ cup (45g) granulated sugar

Pinch of Diamond Crystal kosher salt

4 ounces (113g) unsalted butter,
melted and cooled

To Assemble the Pie

Unbleached all-purpose flour
for rolling the dough

½ recipe Fat + Flour Pie
Dough (page 114), made in
advance and chilled

There are these crazy few weeks every year when all the various stone fruits are ready and ripe and need to be used. That's when I put Stone Fruit Party Pie on the menu. It's definitely a bit of a fruit-cocktail pie, but that's the fun part. Use the best peach, plum, cherry, and apricot options you have available; each type provides a different texture and tartness, and they blend together to create one super stone-fruit pie. A party, if you will. ▶

◀ **Make the filling** Cut the mixed stone fruit into ¾-inch-thick pieces, and combine them with the cherries in a large bowl. Add the bourbon, vanilla bean paste, and lemon zest. Whisk the sugar, salt, cornstarch, and cinnamon together in a small bowl, and add this to the fruit. Toss everything together, so all the fruit is coated.

◀ **Make the crumble topping** Whisk the flour, oats, sugars, and salt together in a medium mixing bowl. Add the melted butter, and mix with a fork until the mixture resembles a buttery crumble.

◀ Preheat your oven to 375°F (190°C). Line a baking sheet with parchment paper.

◀ **Assemble the pie** Lightly flour a work surface. Remove the dough from the fridge, and remove the plastic. If your dough has been chilled overnight, it will need to temper before being rolled; this usually takes 10 to 15 minutes. Once the dough is pliable, roll the disc out to a 12-inch circle. Use flour throughout the rolling process as needed to prevent sticking. Transfer the rolled dough to a 9-inch pie plate, and trim the edge to allow 1 inch of dough to hang over the edge. Roll or fold the hanging edge of the dough over itself, using your thumb and forefinger to crimp the edge. Put the crimped crust into the freezer for 20 minutes.

◀ Once the crust has chilled, pour the filling in, adding all the juices that may have collected in the bottom of the bowl. Scatter the crumble over the top.

◀ Chill the whole pie in the freezer for 10 minutes, transfer it to the prepared baking sheet, then place the pie into your preheated oven, on the center rack, and bake it until the crust is a deep golden brown and the juices from the pie are boiling. This should take 1 full hour, and possibly longer. Cool the pie for 1 hour before eating, to allow the juices to settle and continue thickening. Store any leftovers in the fridge, and warm slices of the cold pie at 375°F (190°C) for 15 minutes before eating, for best results.

Stone Fruit Party Pie

Yellow Peach and Almond Pie

MAKES ONE **9** INCH PIE

For the Filling

¾ cup (150g) granulated sugar

1 teaspoon (3g) Diamond
Crystal kosher salt

3 tablespoons (30g) cornstarch

2 pounds (906g) yellow peaches,
ripe but firm, cut into ¾-inch slices

3 tablespoons (39g) amaretto
(or orgeat or orzata)

1 teaspoon (5g) vanilla bean paste

2 teaspoons (4g) lemon zest

To Assemble the Pie

Unbleached all-purpose flour
for rolling the dough

1 recipe Fat + Flour Pie Dough (page 114),
made in advance and chilled

1 large egg white (33g)

1 teaspoon (13g) amaretto
(or orgeat or orzato)

2 tablespoons (25g) granulated sugar

1 tablespoon (12g) pearl sugar

I've written before that great peaches don't need much to make them sing. A pure peach pie with just sugar and a pinch of salt in a buttery pie crust is, for me, a perfect pie. But, just for fun, I like to mix it up sometimes and add some complementary flavors, like vanilla bean and, in this case, amaretto. The almond flavor of amaretto evokes the sweet but bitter almond scent in the center of the peach pit. If you don't want to buy a whole bottle of amaretto, I suggest using a flavoring syrup like orgeat or orzata—much more affordable and easily found—and they can also be used to make a lovely Italian almond soda during summer to go along with your peach pie! ▶

◀ **Make the filling** Whisk the sugar, salt, and cornstarch together in a medium bowl. Add the peaches, amaretto, vanilla bean paste, and lemon zest and toss so that the peach slices are well coated.

◀ Preheat your oven to 375°F (190°C). Line a baking sheet with parchment paper.

◀ **Assemble the pie** Lightly flour a work surface. Remove the dough from the fridge, and remove the plastic. If your dough has been chilled overnight, it will need to temper before being rolled; this usually takes 10 to 15 minutes. Once the dough is pliable, roll one disc out to a 12-inch circle. Use flour throughout the rolling process as needed to prevent sticking. Transfer the rolled dough to a 9-inch pie plate, and trim the edge to allow 1 inch of dough to hang over the edge. Roll or fold the hanging edge of the dough over itself, using your thumb and forefinger to crimp the edge. Put the crimped crust into the freezer while you roll the top crust.

◄ Lightly flour your work surface again, and roll the second disc of dough out to a 10-inch circle.

◄ Remove the crimped crust from the freezer, and pour the filling in, adding all the juices that may have collected in the bottom of the bowl into the crust. Place the top crust gently over the fruit, and use your thumb to press it into the crimped crust. Cut a few slashes in the top of the pie.

◄ Whisk the egg white, amaretto, and granulated sugar together in a small bowl until the mixture is foamy. Brush the top crust of the pie generously with this, and sprinkle it with the pearl sugar. Chill the whole pie in the freezer for 10 minutes, transfer it to the prepared baking sheet, then place the pie into your preheated oven, on the center rack, and bake it until the crust is a deep golden brown and the juices from the pie are boiling. This should take 1 full hour, and possibly longer. Cool the pie for 2 hours before eating, to allow the juices to settle and continue thickening. Store any leftovers in the fridge, and warm slices of the cold pie at 375°F (190°C) for 15 minutes before eating, for best results.

Caramel Peach Pie

For the Filling

1¼ cups (250g) granulated sugar

3 tablespoons (42g) heavy cream

3 tablespoons (42g) unsalted butter

1 teaspoon (5g) vanilla bean paste

1 teaspoon (3g) Diamond
   Crystal kosher salt

3 tablespoons (30g) cornstarch

2 pounds (906g) yellow peaches,
   ripe but firm, cut into ¾-inch slices

To Assemble the Pie

Unbleached all-purpose flour
   for rolling the dough

1 recipe Fat + Flour Pie Dough (page 114),
   made in advance and chilled

2 tablespoons (28g) heavy cream

2 tablespoons (25g) granulated sugar

One summer, while we were processing all the peaches we had picked at Masumoto Farms, the walk-in broke at the bakery, and because it was summer, the kitchen was incredibly hot. We couldn't leave the peaches out at room temp for fear that they would become overripe. Thinking quickly, we froze the peaches in halves so we wouldn't lose any of them due to the heat. Fast-forward 6 months. Now we needed to make use of these peaches, so, naturally, I said, "Let's thaw them and make some pies." Big mistake: thawing peaches the traditional way causes them to turn a very unappetizing brown. Always trying to think on my feet, I grabbed some butterscotch (brown) and mixed the two together, thinking that, if the peaches were already brown, why not go further brown, ya know? The result was an unexpected harmony that I now look forward to every year. It might not be classic, but it's definitely delicious. ▶

◀ **Make the filling** Measure 1 cup of the granulated sugar, and place it into a medium, heavy-duty saucepan with 2 tablespoons water. Heat the sugar and water over medium heat, stirring constantly with a heatproof spatula. Cook until the mixture is a deep amber-colored liquid. You may start to smell a bit of caramelization; at that point, take the pan off the heat. Add the heavy cream—carefully, because it will sputter and steam aggressively at first. Whisk the cream into the caramel completely, return the pan to the heat, bring the caramel back to a boil, and boil it for 1 minute. Remove the pan from the heat, and transfer the caramel to a heatproof bowl. Add the butter and vanilla bean paste, and whisk until all the butter has been melted and you have a smooth caramel sauce. Allow the caramel to cool for 15 minutes before proceeding with the recipe.

◀ Whisk the remaining ¼ cup granulated sugar, the salt, and cornstarch together in a large bowl. Add the peaches and cooled caramel, and toss so that the fruit is well coated.

◀ Preheat your oven to 375°F (190°C). Line a baking sheet with parchment paper.

◀ **Assemble the pie** Lightly flour a work surface. Remove the dough from the fridge, and remove the plastic. If your dough has been chilled overnight, it will need to temper before being rolled; this usually takes 10 to 15 minutes. Once the dough is pliable, roll one disc out to a 12-inch circle. Use flour throughout the rolling process as needed to prevent sticking. Transfer the rolled dough to a 9-inch pie plate, and trim the edge to allow 1 inch of dough to hang over the edge. Roll or fold the hanging edge of the dough over itself, using your thumb and forefinger to crimp the edge. Put the crimped crust into the freezer while you roll the top crust.

Caramel Peach Pie continues

◄ Lightly flour your work surface again, and roll the second disc of dough out to a 10-inch circle.

◄ Remove the crimped crust from the freezer, and pour the filling in, arranging the fruit so that it's all packed into the crust. Pour all the juices that may have collected in the bottom of the bowl over the fruit. Place the top crust gently over the fruit, and use your thumb to press it into the crimped crust. Cut a few slashes in the top of the pie.

◄ Brush the top crust of the pie generously with the heavy cream, and sprinkle it with the sugar. Chill the whole pie in the freezer for 10 minutes, transfer it to the prepared baking sheet, then place the pie into your preheated oven, on the center rack, and bake it until the crust is a deep golden brown and the juices from the pie are boiling. This should take 1 full hour, and possibly longer. Cool the pie for 2 hours before eating, to allow the juices to settle and continue thickening. Store any leftovers in the fridge, and warm slices of the cold pie at 375°F (190°C) for 15 minutes before eating, for best results.

White Peach and Passion Fruit Pie with Coconut Crumble

MAKES ONE 9 INCH PIE

For the Crumble Topping

1 cup (125g) unbleached all-purpose flour

½ cup (25g) shredded
   unsweetened coconut

¼ cup packed (53g) light-brown sugar

¼ cup (50g) granulated sugar

Pinch of Diamond Crystal kosher salt

4 ounces (113g) unsalted butter,
   melted and cooled

To Assemble the Pie

Unbleached all-purpose flour
   for rolling the dough

½ recipe Fat + Flour Pie
   Dough (page 114), made in
   advance and chilled

For the Filling

¾ cup (150g) granulated sugar

1 teaspoon (3g) Diamond
   Crystal kosher salt

3 tablespoons (30g) cornstarch

2 pounds (906g) white peaches, firm
   but ripe, cut into ¾-inch slices

Juice, pulp, and seeds from
   2 fresh passion fruit

2 teaspoons (4g) grated lemon zest

2 tablespoons (28g) lemon juice

White peaches have a beautiful subtle flavor that is best enjoyed raw—but I have always felt that they lack acid. Though this is not a bad thing necessarily, it can make for a muted pie if not balanced right. Feeling wild one afternoon, I scooped the guts from a fresh passion fruit into a bowl of sliced white peaches, just to see what would become of that pairing, and a new hyper-seasonal classic was born. Succulent, soft white peaches with acidic, floral passion fruit definitely make for an unexpected peach pie; sometimes that's the thing that makes baking fun! ▶

◀ Preheat your oven to 375°F (190°C). Line a baking sheet with parchment paper.

◀ **Make the crumble topping** Whisk the flour, coconut, sugars, and salt together in a medium mixing bowl. Add the melted butter, and mix with a fork until it resembles a buttery crumble. Set it aside.

◀ **Assemble the pie** Lightly flour a work surface. Remove the dough from the fridge, and remove the plastic. If your dough has been chilled overnight, it will need to temper before being rolled; this usually takes 10 to 15 minutes. Once the dough is pliable, roll the disc out to a 12-inch circle. Use flour throughout the rolling process as needed to prevent sticking. Transfer the rolled dough to a 9-inch pie plate, and trim the edge to allow 1 inch of dough to hang over the edge. Roll or fold the hanging edge of the dough over itself, using your thumb and forefinger to crimp the edge. Put the crimped crust into the freezer while you prepare the filling.

◀ **Make the filling** Whisk the sugar, salt, and cornstarch together in a large bowl. Add the peaches, passion fruit innards, lemon zest, and juice and toss so all the fruit is coated. Pour the filling into the crust, along with all the juices that may have collected in the bottom of the bowl. Scatter the crumble over the top.

◀ Chill the whole pie in the freezer for 10 minutes, transfer it to the prepared baking sheet, then place the pie into your preheated oven, on the center rack, and bake it until the crust is a deep golden brown and the juices from the pie are boiling. This should take 1 full hour, and possibly longer. Cool the pie for 1 hour before eating, to allow the juices to settle and continue thickening. Store any leftovers in the fridge, and warm slices of the cold pie at 375°F (190°C) for 15 minutes before eating, for best results.

California Citrus Shaker Pie

For the Citrus Filling

12 ounces (340g) Meyer lemons

1 cup (200g) granulated sugar,
+ more for decorating

3 tablespoons (30g) cornstarch

Pinch of Diamond Crystal kosher salt

2 large egg yolks (34g)

2 large eggs (100g)

1 tablespoon (6g) grated
blood-orange zest

3 tablespoons (39g) blood-orange juice

To Assemble the Pie

Unbleached all-purpose flour
for rolling the dough

1 recipe Fat + Flour Pie Dough (page 114),
made in advance and chilled

3 tablespoons (42g) cold unsalted butter

3 tablespoons (42g) heavy cream

was tempted to stick this pie in the custard chapter, because the filling is in fact a custard, but I have always thought of a Citrus Shaker Pie as a fruit pie—after all, it uses the entire Meyer lemon, skin and all. This pie isn't for everyone; it's textural (a li'l chewy) and rich with citrus essential oils (a li'l bitter). To me, that flavor profile makes it perfect. I like Shaker pies more than citrus curd tarts, but the slicing of the lemons can be frustrating. I prefer to use a serrated knife to tackle that task rather than freeze the lemons, which is another popular trick. This recipe is best made with Meyer lemons, because they have a nice thin skin that bakes well. A thicker-skinned lemon, like Eureka, will not break down enough and will be too chewy. ▶

◀ **Make the citrus filling** Slice the Meyer lemons as thin as you are able to; I like to use a serrated knife for this and take my time, cutting slowly and deliberately. Combine the sliced lemons and sugar in a large nonreactive mixing bowl, cover the bowl with a tea towel or plastic wrap, and let it sit at room temperature for 4 hours, or overnight in the fridge. Remove any seeds that you see; they typically float to the surface once the mixture starts to dissolve the sugar.

◀ Preheat your oven to 375°F (190°C). Line a baking sheet with parchment paper.

◀ **Assemble the pie** Lightly flour a work surface. Remove the dough from the fridge, and remove the plastic. If your dough has been chilled overnight, it will need to temper before being rolled; this usually takes 10 to 15 minutes. Once the dough is pliable, roll one disc out to a 12-inch circle. Use flour throughout the rolling process as needed to prevent sticking. Transfer the rolled dough to a 9-inch pie plate, and trim the edge to allow 1 inch of dough to hang over the edge. Roll or fold the hanging edge of the dough over itself, using your thumb and forefinger to crimp the edge. Put the crimped crust into the freezer.

◀ Lightly flour your work surface again, and roll the second disc of dough out to a 10-inch circle.

◀ Whisk together the cornstarch and salt in a large bowl. Add the egg yolks, and beat the mixture together until it's smooth and creamy. Add the eggs, orange zest, and juice, and whisk to combine everything. Add the sliced lemons and all the syrup that's accumulated around them, and mix gently, so that the fruit is well coated and the syrup has been incorporated into the egg mixture.

California Citrus Shaker Pie continues

◄ Remove the crimped crust from the freezer, and pour the filling in. Break up the butter with your fingers, and dot the surface of the fruit with it. Place the top crust gently over the fruit, and use your thumb to press the top crust into the crimped crust. Cut a few slashes in the top of the pie.

◄ Brush the top crust of the pie generously with the heavy cream, and sprinkle it with sugar. Chill the whole pie in the freezer for 10 minutes, transfer it to the prepared baking sheet, then place the pie into your preheated oven, on the center rack, and bake it until the crust is a deep golden brown and the juices from the pie are boiling. This should take 1 full hour, and possibly longer. Cool the pie for 2 hours before eating, to allow the juices to settle and continue thickening. Store any leftovers in the fridge, and warm slices of the cold pie at 375°F (190°C) for 15 minutes before eating, for best results.

Brambleberry Handpies

MAKES **6** HANDPIES

For the Berry Filling

1 pound (453g) mixed brambleberries
(raspberry, blackberry, boysenberry)

1 cup (200g) granulated sugar,
+ more for decorating

¼ cup (40g) cornstarch

1 tablespoon (6g) grated orange zest

2 tablespoons (26g) orange juice

¼ teaspoon Diamond Crystal kosher salt

To Assemble the Handpies

Unbleached all-purpose flour
for rolling the dough

1 recipe Fat + Flour Pie Dough (page 114),
made in advance and chilled

1 large egg (50g), beaten

Brambleberries are my most-loved fruit subcategory. The name refers to the thorny, intertwined bushes on which these delicate berries grow. They're notoriously hard to harvest; as a result, "brambles" tend to be pricier than easier-to-pick fruit. They are some of my favorite fruits—raspberries, blackberries, boysenberries, marionberries, and tayberries—oh God, they are all so good. Only when they are allowed to ripen fully on the thick stems of the bush—the cane—can their full flavor be enjoyed. Mixed brambleberries stuffed inside a flaky pie-crust pocket is near the top of my list of craveworthy desserts, especially because I know that getting the good brambleberries was such an ordeal. ▶

◀ Combine half of the berries, sugar, cornstarch, orange zest and juice, and salt in a large saucepan, and heat over medium heat until the juices start to release from the fruit and come to a simmer. Stir the fruit often to prevent it from sticking to the bottom of the pan. Continue cooking until the juices thicken to a jammy consistency, about 10 minutes. Remove the filling from the heat, and allow it to cool to room temperature before using it.

◀ Preheat the oven to 375°F (190°C). Line two large baking sheets with parchment paper.

◀ **Assemble the handpies** Lightly flour your work surface, and roll your pie dough out to a rectangle measuring 12 by 18 inches. Cut the rolled dough into six squares.

◄ Once the filling has cooled, add the remaining half of the berries, and stir to combine them. Mound ¼ cup of the filling in the center of each piece of dough, and carefully fold one corner to meet the corner diagonally across from it, forming a triangle-shaped turnover. Use the tines of a fork to close the handpie along the two open sides. Continue with the rest of the filling and pie-dough squares, and place them onto the prepared baking sheets. Poke the tines of the fork into the tops, to provide some ventilation for the filling.

◄ Brush the handpies with the beaten egg, and sprinkle them with sugar. Bake them for about 30 minutes, until the crusts begin to brown. Rotate the pans, and continue baking for 15 more minutes, or until the crusts are a deep golden brown and some juices bubble from the holes on each handpie. Transfer them to a wire rack, and let them cool completely before serving. Store any leftovers in the fridge, and warm the handpies at 375°F (190°C) for 15 minutes before eating, for best results.

Pudding
and Custard
Pies

There's no denying the strong hold that creamy pudding pies have on the dessert world.

I have always been a fan, and what's not to love? Chilled creamy goodness, sometimes with fruit, with even more cream on top? Yes, please! The pudding pie offers a lot of room for experimentation, too, and that's one of my favorite things about this section of the pie roster. It doesn't need to be simply banana or coconut cream. We can do so much more, and I've dreamed up some really special variations on the theme. One innovation in the following recipes for pudding pies is the use of instant pudding mix; at first, this might seem like some trashy vintage hack, but for me it has become a steadfast way to make perfect pudding time and time again, freeing me up to add some extra flavor elements that make each of the pies in this chapter unique.

The classy older sister of the pudding pie has got to be the baked custard pie, in particular the chess or transparent pie, which you'll also find in this chapter. A magical emulsion of eggs, sugar, and butter, this filling style borders on being too sweet, then draws you back in for just one more bite. The most recognizable chess pie will always be pecan, a holiday staple for many pie lovers. Traditionally, bakers differentiate a chess pie from a transparent pie by one single ingredient, cornmeal, which is typically used to thicken a classic chess pie. These days, I find bakers are much looser with the names, and use them interchangeably, the main defining characteristic of both being the high ratio of sugar (or honey) to eggs. ∎

"No-Cook" Puddings

After many years of making cream pies, I have decided one thing: I never need to make an egg-based pastry cream or pudding again. Mastering pastry cream while working in bulk quantities is quite difficult. Once the pudding is made and stored, it's a matter of days before it begins to weep a little, the water leaking from the egg proteins and making the consistency of the pastry cream loose. After that, getting the correct thickness for a pudding-based pie is almost impossible. That is why I switched to no-cook puddings for all of our pudding-based pies. The base of these puddings is the magical modified food starch, which also goes by the name Instant ClearJel, and "instant pudding" when sugar and flavors are added. This starch gels liquids without being heated. In a fruit pie, it will set the fruit juices into a clear, sliceable filling. Mixed into any milk, it creates a quick, eggless pudding. Just adding this starch alone to milk or cream will create a pudding strong enough for a pie, but adding things like ganache or caramel will create something special. ■

Upcycled Broken Cookie Crust

MAKES ONE **9** INCH COOKIE CRUST

1½ cups (150g) cookie crumbs, such as graham crackers, oatmeal cookies, or sugar cookies

2 tablespoons (25g) granulated sugar

4 tablespoons (56g) unsalted butter, melted and cooled

1 teaspoon (3g) Diamond Crystal kosher salt

One of my favorite ways to prepare a cream or custard pie is by upcycling leftover stale cookies into a delicious crust. Crushed cookies or graham crackers mixed with butter, sugar, and a little salt make the perfect base for a creamy, dreamy fridge pie. Here is my basic recipe. ▶

◀ Preheat your oven to 375°F (190°C). Combine the cookie crumbs, sugar, melted butter, and salt in a mixing bowl, and use a spoon to mix them together until you have a moist crumble. Transfer the crumble to a 9-inch pie plate, and press it into the bottom and sides in an even layer.

◀ If your recipe requires a parbaked crust, bake it for 10 minutes on the center rack of the oven, or until the crust is lightly browned at the edges. Remove it from the oven, and proceed with the recipe.

◀ If your recipe requires a fully baked crust, bake the crust on the center rack of the oven for a total of 12 to 15 minutes, until browned all over. Remove the crust from the oven, and cool it completely before proceeding with the recipe.

◀ The cookie-crust mixture can be prepared in advance and stored in a sealed container in the fridge until you are ready to use it; this is the best way to store it, rather than pressing it into the pie plate first.

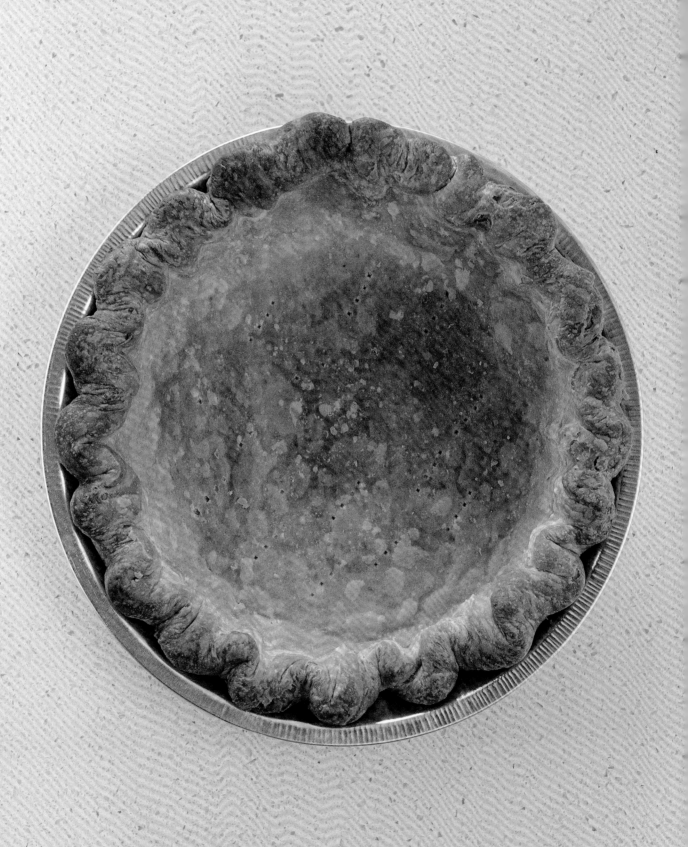

How to Blind-bake a Pie Crust

Blind-baking is simply baker-speak for baking the crust part of the way before assembling the pie. Over the years, I have gathered a lot of data about blind-baking pastry, and I have learned that this is one of the points in the pie process where things are most likely to take a turn for the worse. The biggest issue I see is slumped, underfilled, misshapen crusts. Nine times out of ten, this is the result of two things: using a pastry crust that is too close to room temp when it hits the oven, and underfilling the cavity of the crust with pie weights or beans. Provided that your oven is preheated and you follow the directions below, you will not have a weird, slumped crust—it's nearly impossible for that to happen when the crust is at the correct temp and when there are enough weights or beans pressing into the crust to hold it up.

There are two types of blind-baked crust: parbaked, when the crust is partially baked before adding filling and returning the pie to the oven; and fully baked, when the crust is baked through and then filled with a filling that does not require further cooking. The method for making a perfect parbaked or fully baked crust is all about the prep. Here are the steps to success:

■ Lightly flour a work surface. Remove the dough from the fridge, and remove the plastic. If your dough has been chilled overnight, it will need to temper before being rolled; this usually takes 10 to 15 minutes. Once the dough is pliable, roll the disc out to a 12-inch circle. Use flour throughout the rolling process as needed to prevent sticking. Transfer the rolled dough to a 9-inch pie plate, and trim the edge to allow 1 inch of dough to hang over. Roll or fold the hanging edge of the dough over itself, using your thumb and forefinger to crimp it. Chill the crimped crust in the freezer until it is completely frozen.

■ Preheat your oven to 375°F (190°C). Spray the interior of the frozen crust with nonstick cooking spray, and line it with parchment paper or a large coffee filter. Fill the lined crust with pie weights or dried beans, making sure the weights go all the way up the walls of the plate; this prevents movement and slipping during baking.

■ For a parbaked pastry crust: Place the crust on the center rack of your oven, and bake for 25 minutes, until the edges become golden and the interior crust looks slightly translucent. Remove the crust from the oven and let cool for 15 minutes with the pie weights inside it before gently removing the parchment and weights and proceeding with the recipe.

■ For a fully baked pastry crust: Place the crust on the center rack of your oven, and bake for 30 minutes, until the edges become golden and the interior crust looks slightly translucent. Remove the crust from the oven, gently remove the parchment and weights, and return the crust to the oven to bake for an additional 7 to 10 minutes, until the interior crust is no longer translucent and has begun to take on a little golden color. Cool the crust completely before proceeding with the recipe.

White Chocolate Banana Cream Pie

For the White Chocolate Pudding

⅓ cup (78ml) heavy cream

⅓ cup (56g) roughly chopped
    white chocolate

3.4 ounces (96g) instant
    vanilla pudding mix

1¼ cups (295ml) whole milk

1 teaspoon (5g) vanilla bean paste

Pinch of Diamond Crystal kosher salt

To Assemble the Pie

1 fully baked pie crust (½ recipe Fat +
    Flour Pie Dough, page 114, made in
    advance; see box on page 169)

4 medium (472g) green-tip ripe bananas

1 cup (236ml) heavy cream

2 tablespoons (14g) sifted
    confectioners' sugar

A s much as I have always loved banana cream pie, there was a time when I avoided adding it to my menu, purely because the idea of having to make traditional pastry cream in bulk was so overwhelming. Although it's delicious when made well, traditional pastry cream production for a pie shop can be a pain in the butt; the margin of error for getting the thickness exactly right is slim, and it does not do well in the fridge beyond a few days, thanks to the eggs. The solution to this problem is instant vanilla pudding mix, which is typically just sugar, modified food starch, and vanilla. Used as a base, it creates a strong and fridge-stable pudding that can be gussied up in any number of ways. In this recipe, the pudding is given a silky boost with white chocolate—extra personality. ▶

◀ **Make the pudding** In a medium microwave-safe mixing bowl, heat the cream in your microwave for 1½ minutes, until it's hot but not simmering. Immediately add the white chocolate. Wait 1 minute, and then whisk until the chocolate is melted and the mixture is smooth and thick, like ganache. Set it aside to cool to a warm room temperature.

◀ Place the instant pudding mix into a large mixing bowl. Make a well in the center, and pour in about ⅓ cup (78ml) of the milk.

◀ Whisk vigorously until all the instant pudding mix has been incorporated and no dry lumps remain. Add the cooled chocolate, remaining milk, the vanilla bean paste, and salt, and whisk vigorously until it's thickened, about 2 minutes.

◀ Store the pudding in a sealed container in the fridge until you're ready to use it, or for up to 7 days.

◀ **Assemble the pie** Spread half of the pudding onto the bottom of the crust. Cut the bananas into ¼-inch slices, on the bias. Beginning at the edge of the pie crust, fan the slices of fresh banana in overlapping rows on top of the pudding.

◀ Cover the fresh bananas with the remaining pudding, and smooth it into an even layer. Cover the pie with plastic wrap, and chill it in the fridge while you make the whipped cream, or overnight.

◀ In the bowl of an electric mixer fitted with the whisk attachment, combine the cream and confectioners' sugar, and beat until soft peaks form. Pile the whipped cream on top of the pie, and swoosh it around with the back of a spoon.

◀ Refrigerate the pie for at least 4 hours. When you are ready to serve it, soak a kitchen towel in hot water, and fold it in half. Place the cold pie dish on top of the towel to dislodge the buttery crust from the bottom of the dish, which will make slices of pie easier to remove. Slice the pie using a warm knife, and store any leftovers in the fridge. They will keep for about 3 days.

Vanilla Crunch Cream Pie

MAKES ONE **9** INCH PIE

7 ounces (198g) store-bought crunchy vanilla meringue cookies

1 cup (43g) mini marshmallows

1 batch White Chocolate Pudding (page 171)

1 fully baked pie crust (½ recipe Fat + Flour Pie Dough, page 114, made in advance; see box on page 169)

½ cup (118ml) heavy cream

2 tablespoons (14g) sifted confectioners' sugar

Maraschino cherries, for decoration

This pie is a celebration of vanilla, the magical yet ubiquitous baking ingredient that adds that special something to so many sweet treats. I love vanilla, and this pie is designed to showcase its full range. It uses vanilla bean paste in the pudding, and crunchy meringue cookies, which add texture and the warm flavor of toasted vanilla. This pie is versatile, though, and if you want to shake things up, you could add some really good strawberries or raspberries to the top, or serve them alongside. ▶

◀ Break up the meringues with your hands until they are mostly in 1-inch pieces, with some smaller bits throughout. Add 1 cup of these broken meringues and the mini marshmallows to the pudding, and fold them in. Transfer the filling to the prepared pie crust. Cover the pie with plastic wrap, and chill it in the fridge while you make the whipped cream.

◀ In the bowl of an electric mixer fitted with the whisk attachment, combine the cream and confectioners' sugar, and beat until soft peaks form. Pipe the whipped cream around the edge of the pie; I like to use a large St Honore–shape tip made by Ateco. In lieu of piping the whipped cream, you can pile and swoosh the cream as you like.

◀ Refrigerate the pie for at least 4 hours, or overnight. Top the exposed center of the pie with the remaining meringues, and place the cherries in a border around the edge of the pie just before serving. When you are ready to serve the pie, soak a kitchen towel in hot water, and fold it in half. Place the cold pie dish on top of the towel to dislodge the buttery crust from the bottom of the dish, which will make slices of pie easier to remove. Slice the pie using a warm knife, and store any leftovers in the fridge. They will keep for about 3 days.

Pistachio Ambrosia Pie

For the Ambrosia Filling

½ cup (120g) crème fraîche

1 teaspoon (5g) vanilla bean paste

3.4 ounces (96g) instant pistachio pudding mix

2½ cups (590ml) heavy cream

¼ cup (29g) sifted confectioners' sugar

2 cups (86g) mini marshmallows

1 cup (85g) shredded sweetened coconut

½ cup (60g) roasted salted pistachios, chopped, + more for decoration

11-ounce (312g) can mandarin oranges, drained

8-ounce (227g) can pineapple chunks, drained

To Assemble the Pie

One batch Upcycled Broken Cookie Crust, made of store-bought coconut cookies, fully baked (page 167)

2 cups (330g) lightly sweetened whipped cream (reserved from making the filling)

Maraschino cherries, for decoration

If you love ambrosia, you will enjoy this pie. If you have PTSD from being served ambrosia as a child, you will feel like sending me hate mail. That's how it goes with ambrosia "salad." I love it, and I will die on this mountain of vintage fluff. How do you make ambrosia even better? Well, to start, I use real whipped cream—no Cool Whip shall be found in this pie—and I slather that dreamy filling in a coconut-cookie crust. I love the salted pistachios in this recipe, which provide a contrast to the sweet and squishy pistachio pudding–based ambrosia filling. ▶

◀ **Make the ambrosia filling** In a large mixing bowl, whisk the crème fraîche, vanilla bean paste, and pudding mix together.

◀ In the bowl of an electric mixer fitted with the whisk attachment, combine the cream for the filling and confectioners' sugar, and beat until soft peaks form. Reserve 2 cups (330g) of the whipped cream in a sealed container in the fridge for topping the pie later.

◀ Add the rest of the whipped cream to the pudding, and gently fold it in until no streaks remain. Fold in the marshmallows, coconut, pistachios, oranges, and pineapple.

◀ **Assemble the pie** Transfer the filling to the prepared crust, cover it with plastic wrap, and chill it for 4 hours, or overnight.

◀ Just before serving the pie, top it with the reserved whipped cream, arrange the maraschino cherries in a border around the edge, and sprinkle some pistachios over the whipped cream. Serve the pie immediately. Store any leftovers in the fridge; they will keep for about 3 days. Good luck—I hope your guests love ambrosia.

For the Chocolate Silk Pudding

1 cup (236ml) heavy cream

1½ cups (255g) roughly
chopped 72% chocolate

4 tablespoons (56g) unsalted
butter, at room temperature

5.1 ounces (144g) instant
vanilla pudding mix

½ cup (42g) Dutch-processed
cocoa powder

1 cup (236ml) whole milk

1 teaspoon (5g) vanilla bean paste

Pinch of Diamond Crystal kosher salt

To Assemble the Pie

1 fully baked pie crust (½ recipe Fat +
Flour Pie Dough, page 114, made in
advance; see box on page 169)

1 cup (236ml) heavy cream

2 tablespoons (14g) sifted
confectioners' sugar

hocolate Silk Pie—or French silk, as it was called when I first ate it as a kid—is a luscious alternative to the baked Chocolate Chess Pie recipe on page 192. I love them both, but one of my good friends (Hi, Leiderman!) asked me to make the French silk pie he grew up with for his first birthday party after Covid restrictions were lifted. His benchmark for this pie was from a popular chain restaurant that has since stopped operating, and I riffed on that original recipe to create a pie that was a little quicker and easier to make, but no less chocolatey and rich. ▶

◀ **To make the chocolate silk pudding** In a medium microwave-safe mixing bowl, heat the cream in your microwave for 1½ minutes, until it's hot but not simmering. Immediately add the chocolate. Wait 1 minute, and then whisk until the chocolate is melted and the mixture is smooth and thick, like ganache. Set it aside to cool to a warm room temperature. Add the soft butter, and whisk until it's combined.

◀ Place the instant pudding mix and cocoa into a large mixing bowl. Make a well in the center, and pour in about ⅓ cup (78ml) of the milk.

◀ Whisk vigorously until all the instant pudding mix has been incorporated and no dry lumps remain. Add the remaining milk, the vanilla bean paste, and salt, and whisk vigorously until it's thickened, about 2 minutes. Add the chocolate mixture in three parts, whisking thoroughly between additions, until all the chocolate has been incorporated and no streaks of pudding remain.

◀ **Assemble the pie** Transfer the filling to the prepared pie crust, and smooth the surface with an offset spatula. Cover the pie with plastic wrap, and chill it in the fridge while you make the whipped cream.

◀ In the bowl of an electric mixer fitted with the whisk attachment, combine the cream and confectioners' sugar, and beat until soft peaks form. Top the pie with the whipped cream, and swirl/swoosh it artfully.

◀ Refrigerate the pie for at least 4 hours, or overnight. When you are ready to serve it, soak a kitchen towel in hot water, and fold it in half. Place the cold pie dish on top of the towel to dislodge the buttery crust from the bottom of the dish, which will make slices of pie easier to remove. Slice using a warm knife, and store any leftovers in the fridge. They will keep for about 3 days.

Chocolate Silk Pie

Vegan Chocolate Crème Pie

MAKES ONE 9 INCH PIE

For the Cookie Crust

2 cups (227g) crushed vegan
  chocolate sandwich cookies
  (16 to 20 cookies), such as Oreo

3 tablespoons (42g) unrefined
  extra-virgin coconut oil, melted

For the Pudding

1 cup (236ml) unsweetened
  coconut cream

1½ cups (255g) roughly
  chopped 72% chocolate

2 ounces (57g) vegan cream cheese,
  at room temperature, cut into chunks

5.1 ounces (144g) instant
  vanilla pudding mix

1 cup (236ml) evaporated coconut milk

½ teaspoon vanilla bean paste

Pinch of Diamond Crystal kosher salt

For the Whipped Coconut
Cream Topping

1 cup (236ml) unsweetened
  coconut cream, shaken well
  and refrigerated overnight

¼ cup (28g) sifted confectioners' sugar

This dreamy pie could fool even the biggest vegan-dessert skeptic; there is no loss of texture, flavor, or indulgence when swapping out dairy for the plant-based products in this recipe. The ease with which it comes together is another major plus—no baking necessary! Bonus points if you can get your hands on a chocolate made with coconut sugar, something that's become more popular in recent years; it will impart an extra layer of flavor that takes this pie over the top. ▶

◀ Place the bowl of your stand mixer in the refrigerator to chill for preparing the whipped coconut cream.

◀ **Make the cookie crust** In a medium bowl, stir together the crushed cookies and the coconut oil until the mixture is thoroughly combined and the texture of wet sand. Transfer the cookie crust to a pie pan, and firmly press the crumbs evenly into the bottom and up the sides of the pan. Chill the crust in the freezer while you make the filling.

◀ **Make the pudding** In a medium microwave-safe mixing bowl, heat the coconut cream in your microwave for 1½ minutes, until it's hot but not simmering. Immediately add the chocolate. Wait 1 minute, and then whisk until the chocolate is melted and the mixture is smooth and thick, like ganache. Set it aside to cool to room temperature. Add the cream cheese, and whisk until it's combined.

◀ Place the instant pudding mix into a large mixing bowl. Make a well in the center, and pour in about ⅓ cup (78ml) of the coconut milk. Add the vanilla bean paste and salt.

◄ Whisk vigorously until all the instant pudding mix has been incorporated and no dry lumps remain. Add the chocolate mixture in three parts, whisking thoroughly between additions, until all the chocolate has been incorporated and no streaks of pudding remain.

◄ Transfer the filling to the prepared pie crust, and smooth the surface with an offset spatula. Cover the pie with plastic wrap and place it in the fridge while you make the whipped coconut cream.

◄ **Make the whipped coconut cream topping** Place the cold coconut cream in the chilled mixing bowl. Using your stand mixer fitted with the whisk attachment, whip the cream until the whisk begins to leave tracks in the bowl. Add the confectioners' sugar, and whip until the cream holds a medium-stiff peak. Top the pie with the whipped coconut cream, and swirl/swoosh the cream artfully.

◄ Refrigerate the pie for at least 4 hours, or overnight, and keep it chilled until you're ready to serve it. When you are ready to serve the pie, soak a kitchen towel in hot water and fold it in half. Place the cold pie dish on top of the towel to dislodge the buttery crust from the bottom of the dish, which will make slices of pie easier to remove. Slice using a warm knife, and store any leftovers in the fridge. They will keep for about 3 days.

Butterscotch Cream Pie

MAKES ONE 9 INCH PIE

For the Butterscotch Sauce

1 cup packed (213g) dark-brown sugar

4 ounces (113g) unsalted butter

1 teaspoon (3g) Diamond
   Crystal kosher salt

¼ cup (59ml) heavy cream

3 tablespoons (42g) bourbon

For the Butterscotch Pudding

⅓ cup (78ml) heavy cream

⅓ cup (56g) roughly chopped
   white chocolate

3.4 ounces (96g) instant
   vanilla pudding mix

1¼ cups (295 ml) whole milk

1 teaspoon (5g) vanilla bean paste

Pinch of Diamond Crystal kosher salt

1 cup butterscotch sauce (half
   the recipe above; reserve the
   rest for topping the pie)

To Assemble the Pie

1 fully baked pie crust (½ recipe Fat +
   Flour Pie Dough, page 114, made in
   advance; see box on page 169)

½ cup (118ml) heavy cream

2 tablespoons (14g) sifted
   confectioners' sugar

B utterscotch pudding, or budino, like salted caramel, is a dessert flavor that never loses its popularity. It's often made by cooking a custard in a finnicky hot-water bath, and nailing a perfectly set budino can be hit-or-miss. So I remove the traditional egg-based custard and replace it with instant pudding mix. When you enhance this with homemade butterscotch and add it to a buttery pie crust, you have a pie that is easy to make and impressive to serve. ▶

◀ **Make the butterscotch sauce** Combine the brown sugar and butter in a heavy saucepan over medium heat, and cook just until the sugar is melted. Raise the heat to medium-high, and add the salt and cream. Bring the sauce to a simmer, stirring frequently to keep it from boiling over.

◀ Once the sauce has thickened slightly, add the bourbon, and bring the sauce back to a simmer for 1 minute. Remove it from the heat, and cool completely before using it.

◀ **Make the butterscotch pudding** In a medium microwave-safe mixing bowl, heat the cream in your microwave for 1½ minutes, until it's hot but not simmering. Immediately add the white chocolate. Wait 1 minute, and then whisk until the chocolate is melted and the mixture is smooth and thick, like ganache. Set it aside to cool to a warm room temperature.

◀ Place the instant pudding mix into a large mixing bowl. Make a well in the center, and pour in about ⅓ cup (78ml) of the milk.

◀ Whisk vigorously until all the instant pudding mix has been incorporated and no dry lumps remain. Add the cooled chocolate, remaining milk, vanilla bean paste, salt, and 1 cup of the butterscotch sauce, and whisk vigorously until it's thickened, about 2 minutes.

◄ **Assemble the pie** Transfer the filling to the prepared pie crust, and smooth the surface with an offset spatula. Cover the pie with plastic wrap, and chill it in the fridge while you make the whipped cream.

◄ In the bowl of an electric mixer fitted with the whisk attachment, combine the cream and confectioners' sugar, and beat it until medium-stiff peaks form. Pipe the whipped cream around the edge of the pie; I like to use a large St Honore-shape tip made by Ateco. In lieu of piping the whipped cream, you can pile and swoosh the cream as you like.

◄ Refrigerate the pie for at least 4 hours, or overnight, and keep it chilled until you're ready to serve it. When you are ready to serve the pie, soak a kitchen towel in hot water and fold it in half. Place the cold pie dish on top of the towel to dislodge the buttery crust from the bottom of the dish, which will make slices of pie easier to remove. Slice using a warm knife, and store any leftovers in the fridge. They will keep for about 3 days.

Coconut Cream Pie

For the Coconut–White-Chocolate Pudding

⅓ cup (78ml) heavy cream

⅓ cup (56g) roughly chopped white chocolate

3.4 ounces (96g) instant vanilla pudding mix

1¼ cups (295ml) full-fat coconut milk, well shaken

1 teaspoon (5g) vanilla bean paste

Pinch of Diamond Crystal kosher salt

1½ cups (177g) coconut gel (nata de coco), drained

1 cup (53g) shredded unsweetened coconut

To Assemble the Pie

1 fully baked pie crust (½ recipe Fat + Flour Pie Dough, page 114, made in advance; see box on page 169)

1 cup (236ml) heavy cream

2 tablespoons (14g) sifted confectioners' sugar

As much as I love coconut, I had avoided making and eating Coconut Cream Pie my entire life until I decided I needed to write a recipe for one. And, if I do say so myself, I knocked it out of the park with this rendition, which includes coconut pudding, desiccated coconut, and coconut gel, called "nata de coco," a specialty product that's easy enough to order online or source at your favorite local Asian grocery store. The coconut gel comes in the form of cubes that have a sweet and juicy young coconut flavor to them, a welcome addition to the richness of this cream pie. The snowlike desiccated coconut is an important element here, hydrating in the pudding and creating a sliceable texture. Though this pie is not vegan, it can easily be adjusted by using a nondairy whipped topping, a vegan crust, vegan white chocolate, and coconut cream. ▶

◀ **Make the coconut–white-chocolate pudding** In a medium microwave-safe mixing bowl, heat the cream in your microwave for 1½ minutes, until it's hot but not simmering. Immediately add the white chocolate. Wait 1 minute, and then whisk until the chocolate is melted and the mixture is smooth and thick, like ganache. Set it aside to cool to a warm room temperature.

◀ Place the instant pudding mix into a large mixing bowl. Make a well in the center, and pour in about ⅓ cup (78ml) of the coconut milk.

◀ Whisk vigorously until all the instant pudding mix has been incorporated and no dry lumps remain. Add the cooled chocolate mixture, remaining coconut milk, the vanilla bean paste, and salt, and whisk vigorously until it's thickened, about 2 minutes.

◀ Fold the coconut gel and shredded unsweetened coconut into the thickened pudding.

◀ **Assemble the pie** Transfer the pudding to the prepared pie crust, and smooth the surface with an offset spatula.

◀ In the bowl of an electric mixer fitted with the whisk attachment, combine the cream and confectioners' sugar, and beat until soft peaks form. Pile the whipped cream on top of the pie, and swoosh it around with the back of a spoon.

◀ Refrigerate the pie for at least 4 hours, or overnight, and keep it chilled until you're ready to serve it. When you are ready to serve the pie, soak a kitchen towel in hot water and fold it in half. Place the cold pie dish on top of the towel to dislodge the buttery crust from the bottom of the dish, which will make slices of pie easier to remove. Slice using a warm knife, and store any leftovers in the fridge. They will keep for about 3 days.

Almond Cream Pie

MAKES ONE **9** INCH PIE

For the Almond–White-Chocolate Pudding

⅓ cup (78ml) heavy cream

⅓ cup (56g) roughly chopped white chocolate

½ cup (125g) almond butter (use one made of roasted almonds for best flavor)

3.4 ounces (96g) instant vanilla pudding mix

1¼ cups (295ml) whole milk

1 teaspoon (5g) vanilla bean paste

¼ teaspoon (1g) almond extract

Pinch of Diamond Crystal kosher salt

7 ounces (198g) store-bought crunchy almond meringue cookies, such as amaretti

To Assemble the Pie

1 fully baked pie crust (½ recipe Fat + Flour Pie Dough, page 114, made in advance; see box on page 169)

1 cup (236ml) heavy cream

2 tablespoons (14g) sifted confectioners' sugar

Maraschino cherries, for decoration

Almonds, toasted and chopped, for decoration

A maretti are one of my favorite cookies; I am a big fan of the bitter almond extract, and I love the crunchy-chewy texture. This pie celebrates all the things I love about amaretti, while adding a new layer of texture and flavor with a creamy almond-and-white-chocolate pudding. It's so excellent, and even better with an espresso on the side. ▶

◀ **Make the almond–white-chocolate pudding** In a medium microwave-safe mixing bowl, heat the cream in your microwave for 1½ minutes, until it's hot but not simmering. Immediately add the white chocolate and almond butter. Wait 1 minute, and then whisk until the chocolate is melted and the mixture is smooth and thick, like ganache. Set it aside to cool to a warm room temperature.

◀ Place the instant pudding mix into a large mixing bowl. Make a well in the center, and pour in about ⅓ cup (78ml) of the milk. Whisk vigorously until all the instant pudding mix has been incorporated and no dry lumps remain. Add the cooled chocolate, remaining milk, the vanilla bean paste, almond extract, and salt, and whisk vigorously until it's thickened, about 2 minutes.

◀ Break up the almond cookies with your hands until they are mostly in 1-inch pieces, with some small bits throughout; add them to the pudding, and fold them in.

◀ **Assemble the pie** Transfer the filling to the prepared pie crust. Cover the pie with plastic wrap, and chill it in the fridge while you make the whipped cream.

◄ In the bowl of an electric mixer fitted with the whisk attachment, combine the cream and confectioners' sugar, and beat until soft peaks form. Pile the whipped cream on top of the pie, and swoosh it around with the back of a spoon. Place cherries around the edge of the pie and scatter the almonds over the whipped cream.

◄ Refrigerate the pie for at least 4 hours, or overnight, and keep it chilled until you're ready to serve it. When you are ready to serve the pie, soak a kitchen towel in hot water and fold it in half. Place the cold pie dish on top of the towel to dislodge the buttery crust from the bottom of the dish, which will make slices of pie easier to remove. Slice using a warm knife, and store any leftovers in the fridge. They will keep for about 3 days.

For the Mascarpone–White-Chocolate Pudding

⅓ cup (78ml) heavy cream

⅓ cup (56g) roughly chopped white chocolate

3.4 ounces (96g) instant vanilla pudding mix

1¼ cups (295ml) whole milk

½ cup (120g) mascarpone cheese

1 teaspoon (5g) vanilla bean paste

¼ teaspoon (1g) almond extract

Pinch of Diamond Crystal kosher salt

To Assemble the Pie

1 fully baked pie crust (½ recipe Fat + Flour Pie Dough, page 114, made in advance; see box on page 169)

1 pound (453g) fresh strawberries, sliced, + more for decoration

1 cup (236ml) heavy cream

2 tablespoons (14g) sifted confectioners' sugar

1 ounce (28g) freeze-dried strawberries, crushed to a powder

I f the recipe for Pistachio Ambrosia Pie (page 173) isn't your thing, but you do like fruit and cream anyway, consider this classic combo of sweet strawberries and lightly sweetened cream. The filling in this pie gets an extra zhuzh from some mascarpone cheese, which creates a slightly stiffer pudding to cradle the juicy strawberry slices, and to give some added flair; you can use crushed freeze-dried strawberries for even more strawberry flavor. ▶

◀ **Make the mascarpone–white-chocolate pudding** In a medium microwave-safe mixing bowl, heat the cream in your microwave for 1½ minutes, until it's hot but not simmering. Immediately add the white chocolate. Wait 1 minute, and then whisk until the chocolate is melted and the mixture is smooth and thick, like ganache. Set aside to cool to a warm room temperature.

◀ Place the instant pudding mix into a large mixing bowl. Make a well in the center, and pour in about ⅓ cup (78ml) of the milk. Whisk vigorously until all the instant pudding mix has been incorporated and no dry lumps remain. Add the cooled chocolate, mascarpone cheese, remaining milk, the vanilla bean paste, almond extract, and salt, and whisk vigorously until the mixture is thickened, about 2 minutes.

◀ **Assemble the pie** Transfer half the pudding to the prepared pie crust and add the sliced strawberries, arranging them so they cover the entire surface of the pudding. Add the rest of the pudding, and smooth the surface with an offset spatula. Cover the pie with plastic wrap, and chill it in the fridge while you make the whipped cream.

◀ In the bowl of an electric mixer fitted with the whisk attachment, combine the cream and confectioners' sugar, and beat until soft peaks form. Pile the whipped cream on top of the pie, and swoosh it around with the back of a spoon.

◀ Refrigerate the pie for at least 4 hours. When you are ready to serve the pie, sprinkle the crushed freeze-dried strawberries over the top, and add some fresh strawberries around the edge of the pie. Soak a kitchen towel in hot water and fold it in half. Place the cold pie dish on top of the towel to dislodge the buttery crust from the bottom of the dish, which will make slices of pie easier to remove. Slice using a warm knife, and store any leftovers in the fridge. They will keep for about 3 days.

Strawberry White Chocolate Cream Pie

Lemon Meringue Chess Pie

MAKES ONE 9 INCH PIE

For the Lemon Filling

1¾ cups (350g) granulated sugar

3 tablespoons (30g) finely
   ground yellow cornmeal

3 tablespoons (23g) unbleached
   all-purpose flour

Pinch of Diamond Crystal kosher salt

4 ounces (113g) unsalted butter, melted

5 large eggs (250g)

1 large egg yolk (14g)

1 cup (236ml) fresh lemon juice

1 tablespoon (6g) freshly
   grated lemon zest

To Assemble the Pie

1 parbaked pastry crust (½ recipe Fat +
   Flour Pie Dough, page 114, made in
   advance; see box on page 169)

For the Meringue Topping

3 large egg whites (99g)

1 cup (200g) granulated sugar

Pinch of Diamond Crystal kosher salt

1 teaspoon (5g) apple-cider vinegar

¼ teaspoon (1g) almond
   extract (optional)

emon Meringue Chess Pie absolutely clobbers traditional lemon meringue pie, which is made with that wiggly gel filling. That's because a citrus chess filling has a texture closer to a curd, thanks to the butter and eggs, but is easier to make, because the filling gets cooked in the oven instead of on the stovetop. It has a bright lemon flavor, and a rich, creamy texture. The meringue is a silky and fridge-stable baked cloud on top of the filling. When it's cut properly (carefully), you get that iconic slice of yellow custard and bright white topping. It's a perfect pie to make in the winter, when fresh pie fruits are in short supply (unless you want apples or pears) and you are in search of a bright dessert to wow people. ▶

◀ **Make the lemon filling** Combine the sugar, cornmeal, flour, and salt in a large mixing bowl. Make a well in the center of the flour mixture, and add the melted butter, eggs, and egg yolk. Beat the mixture with a whisk until it's well combined. Add the lemon juice and zest, and beat until the lemon juice has been fully incorporated.

◀ Position a rack in the center of your oven, and preheat to 350°F (176°C). Place your parbaked pastry crust on a parchment-lined baking sheet.

◀ **Assemble the pie** Transfer the filling to the prepared pie crust. Bake it on the center rack of your oven until the filling is puffed at the edges and the center wobbles slightly when touched, 50 to 60 minutes.

◀ Remove the pie from the oven, and increase the oven temperature to 400°F (204°C).

◀ **Make the meringue topping** In the bowl of a stand mixer fitted with the whisk attachment, beat the egg whites on medium-high speed until stiff peaks form. Slowly add the sugar, and beat until all the sugar has dissolved and silky peaks of meringue have formed. Add the salt, vinegar, and almond extract, if using, and beat for 1 additional minute to combine.

◀ Carefully dollop and swoosh the meringue on the surface of the pie. Return the pie to the oven, and bake for an additional 5 to 7 minutes, until the meringue is shiny and lightly browned. As it cools, the meringue will be slightly crunchy on the surface and soft inside. Chill the pie for at least 2 hours before slicing into it. Slice using a warm knife, and store any leftovers in the fridge. They will keep for about 3 days.

For the Tangerine Filling

1¾ cups (350g) granulated sugar

3 tablespoons (30g) finely
ground yellow cornmeal

3 tablespoons (23g) unbleached
all-purpose flour

Pinch of Diamond Crystal kosher salt

4 ounces (113g) unsalted butter, melted

5 large eggs (250g)

1 large egg yolk (14g)

¾ cup (177ml) fresh tangerine juice

¼ cup (59ml) fresh lemon juice

1 tablespoon (6g) freshly
grated tangerine zest

Juice, pulp, and seeds from
2 fresh passion fruit

To Assemble the Pie

1 parbaked pastry crust (½ recipe
Fat + Flour Pie Dough, page 114,
made in advance; see box on page 169)

For the Meringue Topping

3 large egg whites (99g)

1 cup (200g) granulated sugar

Pinch of Diamond Crystal kosher salt

1 teaspoon (5g) apple-cider vinegar

When this pie hits the cold case at the bakery, it goes FAST. Its striking bright-orange color, flecked with black passion fruit seeds and topped with a billow of meringue, makes it hard to miss amongst the other offerings. It tastes just as bright once you dig into a slice. The marriage of tangerine and passion fruit just screams sunshine at you, which is wonderful, since this pie typically gets made during January, after the second round of passion fruit hits the market and we are at the coldest and darkest part of the year. A light in the dark and a treat—can't ask for much more than that from a dessert! ▶

◀ **Make the Tangerine Filling** Combine the sugar, cornmeal, flour, and salt in a large mixing bowl. Make a well in the center of the flour mixture, and add the melted butter, eggs, and egg yolk. Beat the mixture with a whisk until it's well combined. Add the tangerine juice, lemon juice, zest, and passion fruit. Whisk until everything is combined.

◀ Position a rack in the center of your oven, and preheat to 350°F (176°C). Place your parbaked pastry crust on a parchment-lined baking sheet.

◀ **Assemble the pie** Transfer the filling to the prepared pie crust. Bake it on the center rack of your oven until the filling is puffed at the edges and the center wobbles slightly when touched, 50 to 60 minutes. Remove the pie from the oven, and increase the oven temperature to 400°F (204°C).

◀ **Make the meringue topping** In the bowl of a stand mixer fitted with the whisk attachment, beat the egg whites on medium-high speed until stiff peaks form. Slowly add the sugar, and beat until all the sugar has dissolved and silky peaks of meringue have formed. Add the salt and vinegar, and beat for 1 additional minute to combine.

◀ Carefully dollop and swoosh the meringue on the surface of the pie. Return the pie to the oven, and bake for an additional 5 to 7 minutes, until the meringue is shiny and lightly browned. As it cools, the meringue will be slightly crunchy on the surface and soft inside. Chill the pie for at least 2 hours before slicing into it. Slice using a warm knife, and store any leftovers in the fridge. They will keep for about 3 days.

Tangerine Passion Fruit Meringue Chess Pie

Chocolate Chess Pie

MAKES ONE 9 INCH PIE

One batch Upcycled Broken Cookie Crust, using store-bought chocolate cookies, parbaked (page 167)

1 cup (170g) roughly chopped 72% chocolate

1 pound (452g) unsalted butter

2 cups packed (426g) dark-brown sugar

2 tablespoons (11g) Dutch-processed cocoa powder

8 large eggs (400g)

1 teaspoon (3g) Diamond Crystal kosher salt

2 cups (330g) lightly sweetened whipped cream (optional)

Although I began making this pie at the beginning of my pastry career in Los Angeles, to this day I still get emails from customers asking about this particular pie, from that one particular restaurant. The restaurant was Gjusta, and this is the exact recipe I served for my brief time there, which folks still remember eating 15 years later. ▶

◀ Position a rack in the center of your oven, and preheat to 350°F (176°C). Place your parbaked pastry crust on a parchment-lined baking sheet.

◀ Fill a medium pot one-quarter full with water. Set it over medium heat, and bring the water to a simmer. Combine the chocolate and butter in a heatproof bowl, and place it over, but not touching, the simmering water, to create a double boiler. Stir gently until the butter and chocolate are melted and completely incorporated. Remove the bowl, and place it on a dry towel.

◀ In a large mixing bowl, combine the brown sugar, cocoa powder, eggs, and salt. Beat vigorously with a whisk until the mixture is lighter in color and very creamy-looking. Add the warm chocolate, and whisk to combine everything.

◀ Transfer the batter to the prepared crust, and smooth the top. Bake it for 40 minutes, rotate the pan, and continue baking until the batter forms a shiny crust on the surface and jiggles a little bit in the center when tapped, 50 to 60 minutes total. The custard may soufflé during baking; it will collapse once it cools, and that's totally normal. Enjoy the pie warm or chilled, and covered with lightly whipped cream if you wish. Store any leftovers in the fridge; they will keep for about 1 week.

1 parbaked pastry crust (½ recipe Fat +
Flour Pie Dough, page 114, made in
advance; see box on page 169)

4 ounces (113g) unsalted butter,
melted and still warm

¾ cup (255g) wildflower honey

4 large eggs (200g)

½ cup (100g) granulated sugar

1 tablespoon (10g) cornmeal

2 teaspoons (6g) Diamond
Crystal kosher salt

½ cup (118ml) heavy cream

1 teaspoon (5g) vanilla bean paste

1 tablespoon (15g) apple-cider vinegar

1 tablespoon (6g) Earl Grey
tea, pulverized

2 cups (330g) lightly sweetened
whipped cream (optional)

This honey chess pie is a great example of what's called a transparent pie. This style of custard is made with only a little heavy cream, as opposed to other custards, in which cream and milk make up most of the filling. The result is a filling that has a glistening, slightly transparent appearance. Thanks to the small amount of dairy and the high amount of sugar, these types of pies keep well for much longer than creamy pudding-based pies. Which is a good thing, because transparent pies are rich and sweet, and best consumed in slivers rather than slices. ▶

◀ Position a rack in the center of your oven, and preheat to 350°F (176°C). Place your parbaked pastry crust on a parchment-lined baking sheet.

◀ Put the butter into a large mixing bowl, and add the honey; whisk until they're fully combined. Add the eggs, and whisk to combine them. Combine the sugar, cornmeal, and salt in a small bowl, sprinkle this over the honey mixture, and fold the dry ingredients in until no dry bits remain. Add the heavy cream, vanilla bean paste, vinegar, and tea, and whisk to combine everything.

◀ Transfer the filling to the prepared pie crust. Bake it until the filling is puffed at the edges and the center wobbles when touched, 50 to 60 minutes. Cool the pie for at least 2 hours before slicing it. Slice using a warm knife, and serve the pie at room temp or warmed, with whipped cream or a dollop of crème fraîche if you wish. Store any leftovers in the fridge; they will keep for about 1 week.

Honey
Earl Grey
Chess Pie

Owens
Pecan Pie

For the Filling

4 tablespoons (56g) unsalted butter, melted

¼ cup packed (53g) dark-brown sugar

¾ cup (150g) granulated sugar

11 ounces (325g) Lyle's Golden Syrup or agave syrup

4 large eggs (200g)

1 teaspoon (3g) Diamond Crystal kosher salt

2 tablespoons (28g) bourbon (optional, but highly recommended if you enjoy the flavor)

¼ cup (56ml) brewed espresso (optional, but I love it in this recipe)

1 tablespoon (15g) vanilla extract

1 teaspoon (4g) pumpkin pie spice

To Assemble the Pie

1 parbaked pastry crust (½ recipe Fat + Flour Pie Dough, page 114, made in advance; see box on page 169)

2 cups (228g) toasted pecans, crushed (see Note), + more whole pecans for decoration

have done a complete 180° on pecan pie, the most popular transparent pie. For years, I gave it the side-eye and wrote it off as being too sweet, too rich, not my thing. The truth is, I had been burned by a lot of very bad pecan pie. It took a close friend, someone whose taste I trusted, to change my mind. Chris Owens, a bona-fide Texan, presented me with this recipe the second year Fat + Flour was open for Thanksgiving, and I agreed to give it a chance because I trusted Chris. I am so happy I did: even though it still takes me all day and several cups of black coffee to finish one slice, I find myself thinking about it a lot when it's not nearby. I have edited Chris's original recipe a bit to suit the bakery, but I tried to stay true to his vision—truly indulgent, with toasty nuts, a touch of spice, and balanced sweet (but still hella sweet) "goo"— which is a loving technical term for the stuff under the nuts. ▶

◀ Position a rack in the center of your oven and preheat to 350°F (176°C). Place your parbaked pastry crust on a parchment-lined baking sheet.

◀ **Make the filling** Combine all the ingredients for the filling in a blender, and pulse until you have a homogeneous goo. You can also whisk everything together in a bowl, but I've taken to using the blender, because I appreciate the pour spout for filling the pie shell.

◀ **Assemble the pie** Add the crushed pecans to the prepared pie crust. Slowly pour the filling over the nuts; they will float around and rise to the surface on their own, so don't worry too much about how everything looks. Place the whole pecans around the edge of the pie. Bake the pie for 45 to 60 minutes, until the outer 2 inches, at the edge of the custard, puffs a bit but the center is jiggly, like a slightly underfilled water balloon. (Pecan pie filling is a magical sugar custard that has its own center of gravity, so it often looks as if it's NOT done when in fact its specific jiggle is saying, *Take me out of the oven*.) It will continue to bake for a while as it cools. Cool the pie for at least 2 hours before slicing into it. Store any leftovers in the fridge; they will keep for about 1 week.

About chopping pecans versus crushing them: I prefer to toast my nuts until they're fragrant, and then cool them briefly before gently crushing them with the bottom of a measuring cup until they are broken into organic shapes and sizes. You can chop them, sure, but at some point in my career, a chef showed me how easy it was to crush my nuts, and I never went back to trying to wrangle odd-shaped nuts on a cutting board. ∎

Peanut Butter Chess Pie

MAKES ONE 9 INCH PIE

For the Filling

4 ounces (113g) unsalted butter, melted and still warm

¼ cup (60g) smooth peanut butter

¾ cup (255g) wildflower honey

4 large eggs (200g)

½ cup (100g) granulated sugar

2 teaspoons (6g) Diamond Crystal kosher salt

½ cup (118ml) heavy cream

1 teaspoon (5g) vanilla bean paste

1 tablespoon (15g) apple-cider vinegar

To Assemble the Pie

1 parbaked pastry crust (½ recipe Fat + Flour Pie Dough, page 114, made in advance; see box on page 169)

1 cup (142g) chopped peanuts, toasted

2 tablespoons (25g) granulated sugar

2 cups (330g) lightly sweetened whipped cream (optional)

Pecan pie shouldn't be the only chess pie with nuts, especially not when peanuts mingle so excellently with the gooey filling of a chess custard. This is one of my favorite chess pies, because it's got a lot going on—a silky custard deeply flavored with honey and peanut butter, a crunchy sugared peanut top, and a rich butter crust. It gives a peanut-butter-and-chocolate dessert some stiff competition. ▶

◀ Position a rack in the center of your oven and preheat to 350°F (176°C). Place your parbaked pastry crust on a parchment-lined baking sheet.

◀ **Make the filling** Combine all the ingredients for the filling in a blender, and pulse until you have a homogeneous goo. You can also whisk everything together in a bowl, but I've taken to using the blender, because I appreciate the pour spout for filling the pie shell.

◀ **Assemble the pie** Transfer the filling to the prepared pie crust, scatter the chopped peanuts over the filling, and sprinkle the sugar over the top. Bake until the filling is puffed at the edges and the center wobbles when touched, 50 to 60 minutes. Cool the pie for at least 2 hours before slicing it. Slice it using a warm knife, and serve the pie at room temp or warmed, with whipped cream or a dollop of crème fraîche if you wish. Store any leftovers in the fridge; they will keep for about 1 week.

Buttermilk Chess Pie

MAKES ONE **9** INCH PIE

For the Buttermilk Filling

½ cup (62g) unbleached all-purpose flour

2 tablespoons (20g) finely
ground cornmeal

Pinch of Diamond Crystal kosher salt

1 cup (200g) granulated sugar

4 ounces (113g) unsalted butter

4 large eggs (200g),
at room temperature

1¼ cups (295ml) buttermilk,
at room temperature

2 teaspoons (4g) finely
grated orange zest

2 teaspoons (10g) Fiori di Sicilia
extract or orange-blossom water

To Assemble the Pie

1 parbaked pastry crust (½ recipe Fat +
Flour Pie Dough, page 114, made in
advance; see box on page 169)

2 tablespoons (25g) granulated sugar

B uttermilk chess pie won't win any beauty awards. In this version of a chess pie, the filling is no longer glossy and shiny; because of the buttermilk in the recipe, the filling sets up like a browned cheesecake, which can appear a bit boring. But once you have your first bite—preferably still slightly warm from the oven—you will understand that its beauty lies within the tangy and delicately textured custard. A perfect vehicle for berries and other tart fruits, but an underrated star on its own. ▶

◀ Position a rack in the center of your oven, and preheat to 350°F (176°C). Place your parbaked pastry crust on a parchment-lined baking sheet.

◀ **Make the buttermilk filling** Combine the flour, cornmeal, salt, and sugar in a large mixing bowl; set this aside.

◀ In a medium saucepan, warm the butter over low heat, until it's melted and hot but not simmering. Transfer the butter to the flour mixture, and whisk until it's combined. Add the eggs one at a time, beating after each addition until it's well incorporated. Add the buttermilk, orange zest, and extract, and beat until everything is just combined.

◀ **Assemble the pie** Transfer the filling to the prepared pie crust. Sprinkle the sugar over the surface of the pie. Bake until the pie filling is golden and puffed at the edges and the center wobbles slightly when touched, about 1 hour. Cool the pie for at least 2 hours before slicing it. Store any leftovers in the fridge;, they will keep for about 1 week.

Ricotta Pie

MAKES ONE **9** INCH PIE

For the Ricotta Filling

32 ounces (906g) whole-
    milk ricotta, strained

¾ cup (150g) granulated sugar

4 large eggs (200g)

1 teaspoon (5g) lemon juice

1 teaspoon (2g) grated lemon zest

¼ teaspoon (1g) almond extract

To Assemble the Pie

1 parbaked pastry crust (½ recipe Fat +
    Flour Pie Dough, page 114, made in
    advance; see box on page 169)

½ cup (85g) finely chopped
    72% chocolate

½ cup (64g) toasted pistachios,
    chopped, for decoration

Candied orange zest, finely
    chopped, for decoration

Confectioners' sugar, for decoration

This isn't a classic Sicilian ricotta pie; it's what I always wished that pie would be, more like a really great cannoli, with a shattering pastry crust instead of the traditional *pasta frolla* dough. I'm sorry if this very "extra" version offends your nonna. ▶

◀ Position a rack in the center of your oven and preheat to 350°F (176°C). Place your parbaked pastry crust on a parchment-lined baking sheet.

◀ **Make the ricotta filling** Combine all the ingredients for the filling in the carafe of a blender. Blend until the mixture is smooth.

◀ **Assemble the pie** Transfer the filling to the prepared pie crust. Sprinkle the chopped chocolate over the surface of the pie; use a fork or a cake tester to swirl the pieces into the filling. Bake it until the pie filling is lightly golden and puffed at the edges and the center wobbles slightly when touched, about 1 hour. Cool the pie for at least 2 hours.

◀ Once the pie has cooled, scatter the pistachios and candied zest over the top, and dust it with confectioners' sugar just before serving. Store any leftovers in the fridge; they will keep for about 1 week.

Ginger Sweet Potato Meringue Pie

MAKES ONE 9 INCH PIE

For the Sweet-Potato Filling

1 pound (453g) sweet potatoes,
    baked and cooled, skins removed
    (I prefer the Japanese variety)

4 ounces (113g) unsalted butter, melted

1 cup (200g) granulated sugar

1 teaspoon (3g) ground ginger

1 tablespoon (7g) freshly grated ginger

Pinch of Diamond Crystal kosher salt

1 teaspoon (2g) grated lemon zest

2 large eggs (100g)

½ cup (118ml) heavy cream

To Assemble the Pie

1 parbaked pastry crust (½ recipe Fat +
    Flour Pie Dough, page 114, made in
    advance; see box on page 169)

Candied ginger, finely chopped,
    for decoration

2 tablespoons (14g) confectioners'
    sugar, for decoration

For the Meringue Topping

3 large egg whites (99g)

1 cup (200g) granulated sugar

1 teaspoon (5g) apple-cider vinegar

Pinch of Diamond Crystal kosher salt

This is not your grandma's sweet-potato pie. It's spicy, with both ground and fresh ginger, and rich, thanks to butter and heavy cream. Since sweet potatoes are already, well, sweet, it might seem like you're gilding the lily by topping this pie with a billow of meringue, but the two pair perfectly, creating an ethereal version of the holiday classic. ▶

◀ Position a rack in the center of your oven, and preheat to 350°F (176°C). Place your parbaked pastry crust on a parchment-lined baking sheet.

◀ **Make the sweet-potato filling** In the carafe of a blender, combine all the ingredients for the filling, and blend until the mixture is smooth.

◀ **Assemble the pie** Transfer the filling to the prepared pie crust. Bake it on the center rack of your oven until the filling is puffed at the edges and the center wobbles slightly when touched, 50 to 60 minutes. Remove the pie from the oven, and increase the oven temperature to 400°F (204°C).

◀ **Make the meringue topping** In the bowl of a stand mixer fitted with the whisk attachment, beat the egg whites on medium-high speed until stiff peaks form. Slowly add the sugar, and beat until all the sugar has dissolved and silky peaks of meringue have formed. Add the vinegar and a small pinch of salt, and beat for 1 additional minute to combine them.

◀ Return the pie to the oven, and bake for an additional 5 to 7 minutes, until the meringue is shiny and lightly browned. As it cools, the meringue will be slightly crunchy on the surface and soft inside. Chill the pie for at least 2 hours before slicing into it.

◀ Just before serving, scatter the candied ginger over the meringue and dust it with confectioners' sugar. Slice it using a warm knife, and store any leftovers in the fridge. They will keep for about 3 days.

Writing this book has been an absolute pleasure,

thanks to the helpful and patient friends and collaborators I get to work and spend time with every day.

Thank you to my agent and friend, Nicole Tourtelot, for believing I have something unique to say and making sure I am heard.

Thank you to my editor, Tom Pold, and everyone at Alfred A. Knopf for giving me the opportunity to share my ideas.

Thank you, thank you, thank you to Cindi Thompson, who tested every recipe in this book and kept detailed notes with her *honest* opinion.

To Krystle Shelton, Sam Greenspan, Molly Donnellon, and everyone at Fat + Flour, a standing ovation for working so hard, testing recipes, making sure customers know how good the pie is, and supporting whatever crazy idea I dreamed up while I was stoned.

Thank you to Shawn Pham, Molly Millar, and Gillian Ferguson, just a few of my best friends who listened to me work out what this book was and never once told me to shut up.

To my good friends and often inspiration, Cheryl and Griff Day, for all our intense cookbook discussions, recipe trading, and friendship—thank you, thank you, thank you.

Thank you to Alan Gastelum for helping me shape the creative vision of this book with your photos and flexible work style ☺.

Thank you to my husband and my favorite person, Blaine Rucker. I love you. A very smart person once told me, "Bake all the beautiful cakes, write all the beautiful songs, and make lots of art." And it is not something I take for granted that every day I get to do some of those things as my JOB. How lucky am I?

Acks

(Page references in *italics* refer to illustrations.)

A NOTE ON THE TYPE

This book was set in Geograph, designed by Kris Sowersby (b. 1981)
and published by the Klim Type Foundry in 2019. A contemporary, geometric
sans serif originally designed for *National Geographic*, Geograph draws
upon the idealism of Futura and the pragmatism of Super Grotesk.

Composed by North Market Street Graphics, Lancaster, Pennsylvania

Printed and bound by C&C Offset, China

Designed by Anna B. Knighton

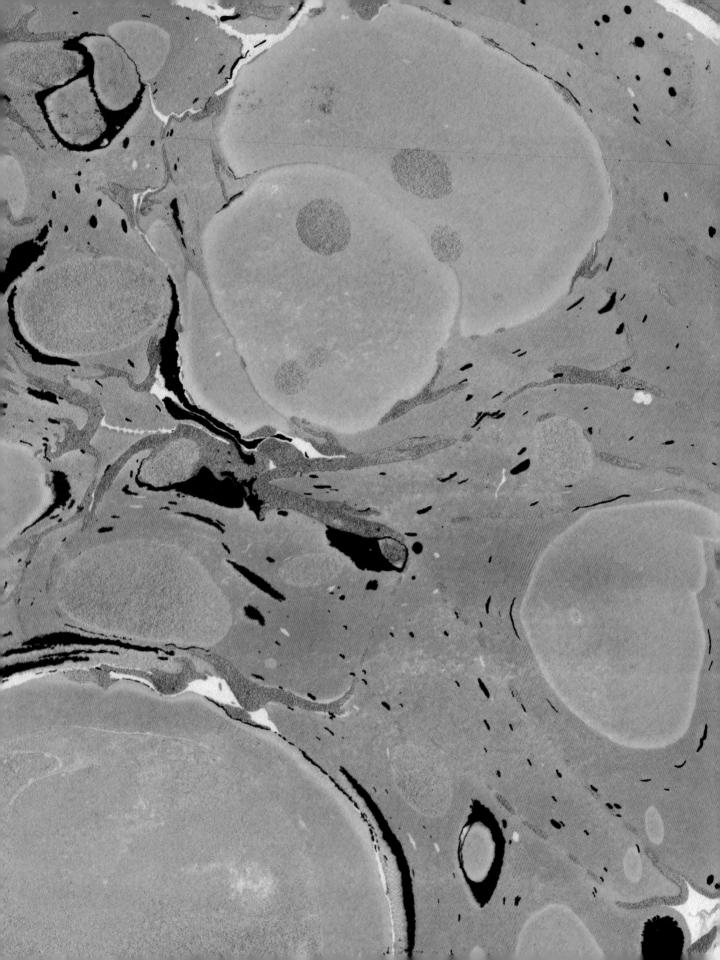

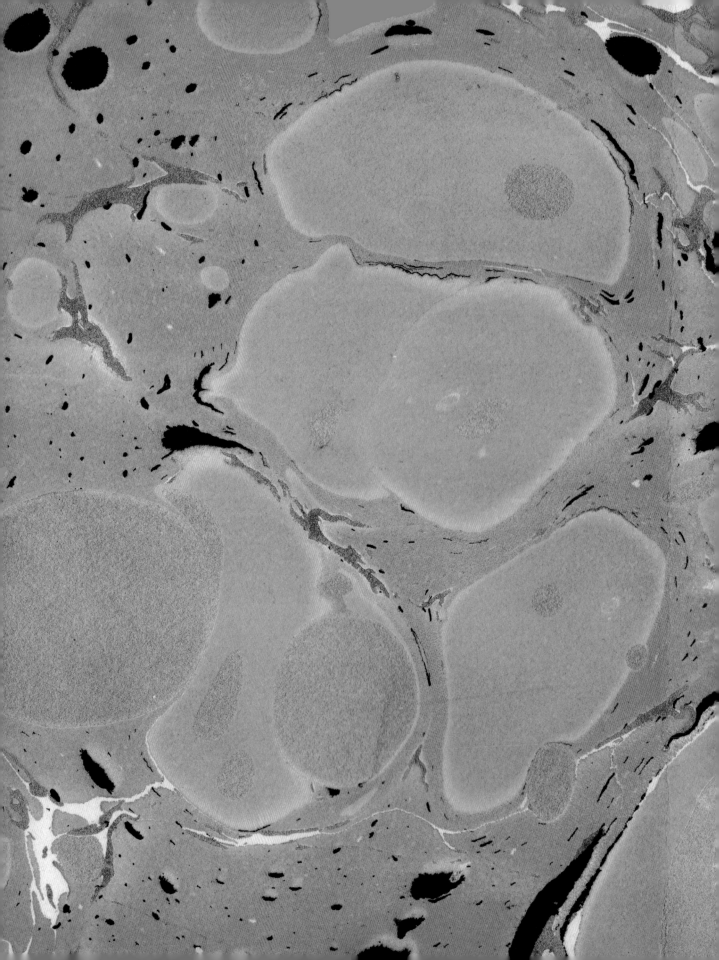